Russian Tortoises as pets.

The Russian Tortoise: facts and information.

Daily care, pros and cons, cages, heating, costs, diet and breeding all covered.

by

George Hoppendale

Table of Contents

Foreword...7

Acknowledgements 11

Chapter 1: Introduction to the Russian Tortoise 12

1. Basic Description and Biology 12
   a) External Features 12
   b) Internal Anatomy 15
   c) Size, Growth Rate and Longevity........................ 17

2. Terminology and Classification 18
   a) Terminology 18
   b) Classification 19

3. Range, Natural Habitat and Status in the Wild.............. 21
   a) Range... 21
   b) Natural Habitat 21
   c) Status in the Wild 21

4. Ecology... 22
   a) Basic Principles of Ecology 22
   b) Russian Tortoise Feeding Ecology 22
   c) Predators of Russian Tortoises 24
   d) Other Interspecific Interactions 24

5. Behavior and Social Structure 24

Chapter 2: Russian Tortoises as Pets...............................28

1. The Pros and Cons of Russian Tortoises as Pets (Considerations for Prospective Keepers) 28

2. Keeper Responsibilities.................................... 29

3. Costs... 30
   a) Typical Costs... 30
   b) Practical Cost Saving Measures......................... 32

4. Myths and Misunderstandings.............................. 33

Table of Contents

Chapter 3: Captive Care **38**

1. What You Need 38

2. The Enclosure 38
   a) Outdoor Caging 39
   b) Indoor Caging 44

3. Keeping Multiple Animals in the Same Habitat 46

4. Lighting 48

5. Heating 52
   a) Ambient Temperatures and Surface Temperatures 53
   b) Thermal Gradients 53
   c) Adjusting the Cage Temperatures 54

6. Substrates 56

7. Cage Décor and Furniture 57

8. Cage Maintenance 58
   a) Daily Tasks 59
   b) Monthly Tasks 59
   c) Annual Tasks 60
   d) Cleaning Techniques and Products 60
   e) During Maintenance 60

Chapter 4: Annual Cycles and Brumation (Hibernation) **62**

Chapter 5: Food and Supplements **66**

1. The Basics of the Diet 66

2. The Importance of Variety 67

3. Feeding Frequency and Quantity 68

4. Important Aspects of Dietary Chemistry 69
   a) Calcium and Phosphorus 69
   b) Oxalates, Phytic Acid and Goiterogens 69

5. Developing the Menu 70

6. Good Foods for Russian Tortoises 70
   a) Leaves, Weeds and Flowers 70
   b) Grasses 71

Table of Contents

c) Grocery Store Vegetables 72

d) Fruits 73

7. Toxic Plants 73

8. Supplements 78

Chapter 6: Water **80**

1. Drinking 81

2. Soaking 82

3. Misting 83

Chapter 7: Interacting With Your Turtle **85**

1. Stress 85

2. Handling Your Pet 87

3. Transporting Your Tortoise 88

4. Outings (aka "Field Trips" or "Turtle Walks") 89

5. Hygiene and the Handler 90

Chapter 8: Breeding **92**

1. To Breed, or Not to Breed? 92

2. Distinguishing Males from Females 93

3. Assembling a Breeding Group 94

4. Preparations and Pre-Breeding Conditioning 95

5. Mating 96

6. Egg Deposition 96

7. Postpartum Female Care 97

8. Egg Incubation 98

9. Care of the Hatchlings 100

Chapter 9: Veterinary Care **103**

1. Finding a Good Tortoise Veterinarian 103

Table of Contents

2. Common Health Problems and Their Resolutions 104

  a) Respiratory Infections 104

  b) Parasite Issues.. 106

  c) Nutritional Problems 107

  d) Traumatic Injuries 109

3. Keys to Good Health.. 110

Chapter 10: Acquiring a Russian Tortoise................................112

1. Captive Bred vs. Wild Caught 112

2. Places to Purchase or Adopt Russian Tortoises 113

  a) Breeders 113

  b) Pet Stores... 114

  c) Pet Expos and Swap Meets 115

  d) Online Markets.. 116

  e) Reptile Rescues and Similar Organizations 116

3. The Quarantine Process 117

4. Legal Considerations 119

Chapter 11: Resources, Support and Further Reading................120

1. Books.. 120

  a) General Reptile Books 121

  b) Turtle and Tortoise Books 121

  c) Russian Tortoise Books 122

2. Informative Websites, Message Boards and Forums.............. 123

  a) General Turtle and Tortoise Sites............................... 123

  b) Russian Tortoise Sites 124

  c) Central Asia Geographic and Climate Information 126

3. Clubs and Organizations 126

4. Conservation Groups, Academic Institutions and Information 128

5. Veterinarians, Health Resources and Husbandry Supplies.................. 129

References...131

Index 132

Foreword

Caring for exotic animals, such as reptiles and amphibians, is a completely different endeavor to keeping domestic pets. While the former usually hail from faraway lands, possess bizarre biological features and subsist on foods humans could hardly fathom; humans have deliberately altered the characteristics of dogs, cats and horses to make them better companions and easier to care for.

This has essentially removed the mystery from husbanding these domestic animals; there are few "great mysteries" surrounding the care of dogs and cats. Dogs and cats can live long, healthy lives feeding exclusively on commercially produced diets and many will even beg for human food as well. Information about dogs and cats is easy to find, and virtually every licensed veterinarian is qualified to treat them. Dogs and cats are generally content to enjoy the same houses as their human owners, and in many ways, become members of human families.

By contrast, the keeping of exotic species is an activity riddled with questions and challenges. While a few commonly kept species have time-tested recipes that lead to success, the needs of most exotic animals are poorly understood. Their foods are often difficult to acquire and expensive. Finding high-quality information about reptiles and amphibians is difficult, as is finding a veterinarian qualified to treat them.

Many endangered reptiles and amphibians are difficult for professional zookeepers to maintain, despite their years of experience and substantial financial commitment. Captive reproduction is an even more difficult goal to achieve, and some species have never successfully reproduced in captivity.

For those who wish to keep exotic animals, this presents a series of challenges. Such keepers must strive to give their unusual pets a high quality of life, even when the factors that contribute to such a life are largely unknown. The most appropriate strategy for beginners is to choose a species and specimen that offers as few challenges as possible, thus increasing the odds of success.

However, keepers have developed successful approaches for many exotic species that do not make good pets. Most experienced keepers can easily care for a reticulated python (*Python reticulatus*), but that does not mean a snake that reaches 15 feet (4.5 meters) or more in length is an appropriate animal to keep in a residential home. Likewise, experienced keepers can maintain green iguanas relatively easily, but their size, disposition and care requirements are too daunting to make them good pets for most people.

Nevertheless, many exotic species have both well-established husbandry protocols and characteristics that make them good pets. Bearded dragons (*Pogona vitticeps*), leopard geckos (*Eublepharis macularius*) and ball pythons (*Python regius*) are all examples of such species. These and many others are regularly bred in captivity, very hardy, docile and they do not reach large sizes.

Currently, few tortoises meet all of these criteria. While African spurred tortoises (*Geochelone sulcata*) are bred with regularity and their husbandry requirements are well understood, they will eventually grow into 100-pound (45 kilogram) behemoths. Red-footed tortoises (*Chelonoidis carbonaria*) are almost as easy to keep, but they are also large, reaching about 15 inches (30 centimeters) in length, thus requiring very large habitats.

While there are many species of tortoise that do stay small, such as pancake tortoises (*Malacochersus tornieri*) and some of the Mediterranean tortoise (*Testudo* spp.), they are often expensive and ill suited for beginners.

One species that does stay small and has a relatively well-established husbandry protocol is the Russian tortoise (*Testudo horsfieldii*). While there are still many questions surrounding their care, they are generally well adapted for captivity and are bred with increasing regularity. Dedicated beginners have a great chance of success with the species.

Nevertheless, keepers of Russian tortoises must be prepared to solve husbandry challenges and learn as much as they can about the species. This includes communicating and learning from other keepers as well as learning about the animals in the wild and their natural habitat. Unfortunately, little research has focused on the lives of these animals in the wild. When researchers do have the opportunity to study these animals, their goals are usually conservation-oriented, and may produce little helpful data for keepers of the species.

A 2002 study of Russian tortoises, published in the Canadian Journal of Zoology, illustrates this well. According to the study, Russian tortoises are "probably the most widespread and abundant of all living terrestrial tortoises, but paradoxically, this chelonian has been studied only superficially." (Frédéric Lagarde, 2002)

When researchers have conducted studies of these tortoises, they have often produced startling results. For example, studies that took place at the beginning of the 21st century showed that these tortoises do not appear to eat many grasses at all; a finding that was at odds with the long held view that grasses were a primary staple of their diets. (Fre´de´ric Lagarde, 2003)

For those who wish to keep Russian tortoises or any other poorly known exotic species, this paucity of information can be frustrating. How can amateur tortoise enthusiasts be expected to provide quality care for animals whose natural history is so poorly understood?

The two-part answer is simple, but the potential results are profound. Initially, keepers should learn the strategies of those who have succeeded with the tortoises in the past, and mimic the husbandry protocols and captive conditions that have been proven to work.

Once a new keeper has a grasp of the basics, he or she gets to join other, similar keepers all over the world as they share ideas, successes and failures, to provide better care for their captives. Many advances in exotic animal husbandry have come from the minds and hearts of amateurs, who may have been a little more observant or a little more creative than the masses.

Caring for exotic animals is challenging, and unlike the care of domestic animals, there is much to be learned. However, by standing on the shoulders of those with more experience, learning everything you can about the species you keep and remaining dedicated to your exotic pet, you may one day discover a solution to a husbandry problem, figure out the explanation for bizarre behavior or even make observations that help conservationists protect the species in the wild.

Acknowledgements

Thanks to my dad for bringing me up around animals.

To my wife and children, a big thank you for supporting me in whatever I do.

Chapter 1: Introduction to the Russian Tortoise

Russian tortoises (*Testudo horsfieldii*) are small, terrestrial, herbivorous reptiles that inhabit Central Asia. Known by several different names, Russian tortoises are also known as Horsefield's, Four-toed, Afghan and Asian steppe tortoises. Some people even refer to them as Russian box turtles. Those who keep these remarkable creatures affectionately call them "horseys," as a shorthand reference to their scientific name.

1. Basic Description and Biology

While Russian tortoises are physically unremarkable relative to other tortoises, they share a number of bizarre morphological traits with their relatives, which are unique in the Animal Kingdom.

a) External Features
Russian tortoises are round in shape when viewed from above, but they appear flattened when viewed from the front or back. This low, round shell design is an adaptation that helps them to construct and move through burrows in their natural habitat. The shell's low profile makes it easier for the tortoises to tunnel and dig than it would be if they had the highly domed shells of some of their close relatives, such as the Mediterranean tortoises. Their round shape also makes it easier for them to turn around in the tight confines of their burrows. (X. Bonnet, 2008)

The shell of Russian tortoises forms from the fusion of dermal bones, which originate within the tortoise's skin, with the ribs and spine. Scale-like structures called scutes cover the top of this bony, box-like frame. Scutes are composed of keratin - the same substance that forms human fingernails and hair.

The top portion of the shell is called the carapace, while the bottom portion of the shell is called the plastron. The scutes that encircle the shell's rim are called marginal scutes. Russian tortoises have 13 dorsal scutes, 12 ventral scutes and 22 marginal scutes. There is no hinge on the shell of Russian tortoises, as there is with some other small and medium-sized chelonians.

Turtles and tortoises replace and shed the scutes covering their shells regularly. New keratin scutes are added from the bottom, as the outermost (and oldest) scutes fall off.

Russian tortoise carapaces are variably colored, and they may appear yellow, brown, yellow-green or horn-colored. Some specimens have prominent black markings on their carapace and plastron, while others only have markings on their carapace, and others still are devoid of such markings completely. Their heads, neck, legs, tail and feet are usually some shade of brown or yellow, often with dark markings or mottled areas. The shell and areas of exposed skin are dry to the touch.

The heads of Russian tortoises hold their two large, endearing eyes. Like most turtles and tortoises, Russian tortoises possess good eyesight, and rely on it for finding food. Like all other living tortoises, Russian tortoises have no teeth; instead, they use their sharp, beak-like mouths to cut and tear food into pieces small enough for swallowing. Russian tortoises have small sensory structures in the roof of their mouth, behind the edge of the beak. (Marcela Buchtová, 2009) Scientists do not yet fully understand the function of these structures, but it probably helps the tortoises to manipulate food while it is in the mouth.

Russian tortoises have no external ear opening, and while they do react to auditory stimuli, they probably do not hear very well. Most turtles are mute, but some tortoises – including male

Russian tortoises – make high-pitched grunting or clucking sounds while courting or breeding females. Russian tortoises have two nostrils on the front of their head, and they possess a good sense of smell. Tortoises, like most other vertebrates, can breathe through both their nostrils and mouth.

Russian tortoises have four strong legs that are well adapted for hauling their heavy bodies through the habitat. Called elephantine feet, these strong, pillar-like legs are an important adaptation for animals that must transport such massive skeletons. The feet of Russian tortoises bear four nails – a unique feature within their genes. Additionally, the bones in their feet are much different from those of their close relatives – another adaptation for their burrowing lifestyle. (Ellen Hitschfeld, 2008)

When threatened by a predator, Russian tortoises will withdraw their heads and cover their faces with their front legs. As their legs are covered in hard, protective scales, they help to provide additional protection from predators.

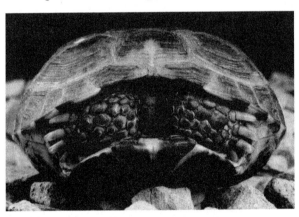

Note the thick scales that protect the Russian tortoise's legs and the four toes on the feet.

While male and female Russian tortoises have differently configured tails – those of males are much longer than females and feature a different positioning of the vent – neither of the sexes have especially long tails. The tip of the tail bears a very small, horny spike of unknown function.

b) Internal Anatomy

Internally, Russian tortoises feature anatomy that is largely similar to that of other terrestrial vertebrates, and contains largely the same basic systems. The skeletal and muscular systems of Russian tortoises provide them with structure and the capacity for movement. Their digestive and excretory systems nourish their bodies, while their endocrine and exocrine systems produce hormones and other substances to ensure their bodies function normally. Their nervous systems transmit information and control the movements of their bodies.

The skeleton of Russian tortoises resembles that of other four-legged vertebrates, aside from the drastically modified spine and ribs. Additionally, tortoises possess anatomical modifications, such as modifications to the bones of the shoulders and pelvis, which allow them to pack most of their body inside their rib cages – a condition unique to chelonians.

Turtles breathe air, just as all other reptiles do. They inhale air through the lungs or mouth, where it travels via the windpipe or trachea to a pair of lungs. The tracheas of turtles are longer than those of similarly sized vertebrates because air has to travel the length of their relatively long necks. In the lungs, the turtles oxygenate the blood and remove the carbon dioxide that it is carrying, at which point it can be exhaled through the mouth or nose.

However, the pulmonary system of turtles does have one key difference from those of birds and mammals – reptiles lack a diaphragm. The diaphragms of birds and mammals pump air into and out of the lungs, while reptiles use muscles attached to the ribs to help pump air into and out of the lungs.

Animals such as lizards and snakes move their ribs, which in turn pump air into and out of the lungs. However, turtles and tortoises cannot move their ribs, as the ribs are attached to their rigid shells. Turtles and tortoises overcame this problem by evolving sheets of muscle within their ribs, which alternately contract and relax to force air into or out of the lungs. Additionally, when turtles move their legs it can create a pumping effect in the lungs as well, which increases the rate of air exchange.

The circulatory system of Russian tortoises and other turtles is largely similar to those of other vertebrates. The heart pumps blood to the body's various tissues by using a circuit of arteries, veins and capillaries. However, in contrast to mammals and birds, turtles have a three, rather than four, chambered heart. Turtle hearts have a left atrium, a right atrium and a single ventricle.

Three-chambered hearts are not as efficient at keeping oxygen-rich blood separate from oxygen-depleted blood. However, turtles have overcome this in part by evolving a muscular septum that partially separates the ventricle into two halves. This improves the efficiency of the heart somewhat, but still limits the aerobic capacity of turtles, meaning that they tire quickly after strenuous activity.

The digestive systems of Russian tortoises and their kin are similar to those of other vertebrates, but there are a few exceptions. The stomachs of turtles usually reside significantly to the left of their midline, and the intestines are compressed into a small amount of space. The process by which turtles handle nitrogenous waste differs from that of mammals, but anatomically, the kidneys and urinary tract are largely similar to the familiar system found in mammals. However, in reptiles, the urinary by-products are excreted via a structure termed the cloaca. The cloaca is a shared chamber, into which the digestive, urinary and reproductive tracts empty.

The gonads of male turtles and tortoises are rather similar to the ones found in mammals, but they are held internally. Male turtles produce sperm in their testes and use a phallus, which arises as an outgrowth of the cloacal wall, to implant sperm in a female's cloaca. The phallus is held inside the cloaca until it is time for mating.

Female tortoises produce ova in their ovaries; after release and fertilization, the eggs settle into a structure termed the oviduct to complete their development. At this time, the mother's body begins placing calcium around the ova to establish their shells. When the eggs are ready for deposition, they are passed through the female's cloaca, one at a time.

While the nervous system of Russian tortoises follows the same basic plan as is found in other vertebrates, tortoises are noteworthy for having very small brains. Usually, the brain of a tortoise is less than one percent of its total mass.

c) Size, Growth Rate and Longevity

Russian Tortoises are relatively small by tortoise standards. At the time of hatching, most Russian tortoises are about one inch in length (2.5 centimeters). As adults, they range from about 6 to 8 inches (15 to 20 centimeters) in straight-line shell length. Females attain larger sizes than males do, and occasionally achieve 10 inches (25 centimeters) in total length. Adult Russian tortoises weigh up to about 1.25 pounds (600 grams), although large individuals may weigh more than this.

Russian tortoises are slow growing, and it takes them about a decade to mature. In captivity, they can reach about 5 to 6 inches (12 to 15 centimeters) in length over a period of 10 to 12 years, if fed an appropriate diet. It is possible to achieve more rapid growth by feeding animal protein, but this is a horrible practice that usually results in nutritional problems later in life.

Russian tortoises have life spans that average from 40 to 50 years. Illness, parasites and predators may shorten this in some cases, but captive Russian tortoises may live much longer under ideal conditions. Ultimately, it remains to be seen how long Russian tortoises can live when well cared for.

2. Terminology and Classification

a) Terminology
The terms "turtle," "tortoise," "terrapin" and "chelonian" are not always applied consistently, and some clarification is warranted.

The term "turtle" correctly refers to all 327 currently recognized species of the order Testudines. Likewise, the term "chelonian," refers to all living turtles – this term arose from the word "Chelonia," which is an outdated name for the order. This means that the terms "turtle" and "chelonian" apply to sea turtles, leopard tortoises (*Geochelone pardalis*), red-eared sliders (*Trachemys scripta elegans*) and all of their close relatives.

The term "tortoise" applies to land-dwelling, herbivorous species of the family Testudinidae, although some people use the term to describe any terrestrial turtle. For instance, rather than calling a *Terrapene carolina* an eastern box turtle, some call it a eastern box tortoise. This is not technically correct, but it is common to encounter such usage.

The term "terrapin" applies to freshwater turtles, although it may refer specifically to one species: the diamondback terrapin (*Malaclemys terrapin*). This term is most common in the southeastern United States as well as along the Mid-Atlantic coast. In some places, the term refers to aquatic turtles that are commonly consumed by humans – in such cases; it may be applied to sliders (*Trachemys* sp.), cooters (*Pseudemys* sp.) or even common snapping turtles (*Chelydra serpentina*)

Therefore, while the name "Russian tortoise" is one of the most descriptive, informative and accurate common names for these creatures, the name "Russian turtle" is also acceptable. "Russian terrapin" is not an appropriate name for these creatures, but the generic terms turtle, tortoise and chelonian are all applicable. However, as this species is found over a large range that includes many different countries, the best possible name for the species is "Central Asian Tortoise."

b) Classification

Scientists do not completely agree on the classification scheme for turtles. While scientists do agree that all turtles are related, they disagree about where their common ancestor fits in the vertebrate family tree. Some researchers are convinced by DNA-based evidence that suggests that chelonians' closest relatives are animals called archosaurs – a group that included dinosaurs and pterosaurs, but is represented by birds and crocodilians in the modern world. By contrast, other researchers find the morphological evidence more compelling, and believe that lizards are the closest relatives of turtles.

Regardless of which point of origin scientists eventually agree upon, turtles are clearly a monophyletic group, meaning that they all arose from a common ancestor. The shell of turtles is one of the most unique adaptations that any animal has ever evolved, and it is highly unlikely that this adaptation evolved more than once.

The basal split in the chelonian lineage is between those turtles whose necks fold sideways, and those whose necks retract vertically, straight back into the ribcage. Most living species have vertically retracting necks, and scientists recognize several subgroups of this group. One such group is the family testudinidae, which contains all of the living tortoises. Scientists divide these different tortoises into different genera, each of which contains one or more species. Russian tortoises belong to the genus *Testudo*.

Russian tortoises were officially described in 1844, by British researcher J. E. Gray, though native people of the region were undoubtedly familiar with the species for thousands of years prior to this. Gray named the species *Testudo horsfieldii* in honor of the American naturalist Thomas Horsfield.

In 1966, some scientists created a new genus – *Agrionemys* – solely for the Russian tortoise. This was based on the number of morphological differences between Russian tortoises and their Mediterranean relatives in the genus Testudo, including the differing bones of the foot, number of claws on the feet and peculiarities of the shell. However, most authorities have reverted to the original classification, and they place the species in the genus *Testudo*. As a hobbyist, you must be familiar with both scientific names to ensure you can find all of the relevant research on the species.

Many authorities recognize three subspecies of the Russian tortoise, but the taxonomy of the species is far from resolved. In 2009, studies of Russian tortoise mitochondrial DNA revealed that there were at least three different types of Russian tortoises; but the genetic differences are not consistent with the three recognized subspecies! (Uwe Fritz, 2009)

While the differences between the three recognized subspecies are subtle and of little importance to the average pet owner, some may enjoy knowing the subspecies they possess. The basic biology and behavior for all three subspecies is similar.

- Central Asian tortoises (*Testudo horsfieldii horsfieldii*) are the lightest colored subspecies, and are usually yellow with scattered dark mottling. The Central Asian tortoise also has the largest carapace of the three subspecies.
- Kazakhstan Tortoises (*T. h. kazachstanica*) are more rectangular than the other subspecies are, and they have more dark markings on their carapaces.
- Kopet-Dag Tortoises (*T. h. rustamovi*) have small, rectangular carapaces and only inhabit southwestern Turkmenistan and western Kazakhstan.

According to several authorities, most specimens in the United States and European collections appear to be of the subspecies *T.h.kazachstanica*, which originated in Uzbekistan.

3. Range, Natural Habitat and Status in the Wild

a) Range

Russian tortoises hail from southeastern Russia, Kazakhstan, Turkmenistan, Uzbekistan, Iran, Pakistan, Afghanistan and China. The area falls between about 45 and 35 degrees North Latitude. The Russian tortoise range borders the Caspian Sea to the West and the Himalayas and Gobi Desert to the East. The climate of this region is very harsh, featuring very long, cold winters and long, hot summers. The transitional seasons between the summer and winter are very short. Russian tortoises often inhabit upland areas that are over 5,000 feet (1500 meters) above sea level.

b) Natural Habitat

The Central Asian Steppe covers the northern reaches of this range, while the southern portion of the range is composed primarily of deserts and arid, mountainous regions. Nutrient poor soils, flat plains and gently rolling topography characterize the steppe. The area receives enough rain to sustain short grasses, but not enough to support tall grasses or trees. The soil is loamy, but deficient in nutrients.

In the southern portion of the range, scattered oases punctuate vast areas of barren, rocky landscapes. These areas hold more lush vegetation, and Russian tortoises tend to aggregate in such places. In the northern portions of their range, the turtles tend to occur at lower densities.

c) Status in the Wild

The IUCN Red List of threatened species lists Russian tortoises as "Vulnerable" in the wild. (IUCN Red List of Threatened Species, 2014) Their primary threats in the wild are habitat destruction and collection for the pet trade. (Frédéric Lagarde, 2002). Habitat destruction chiefly occurs as portions of the Russian tortoise's habitat are converted to agricultural fields.

4. Ecology

a) Basic Principles of Ecology

No animal exists in a vacuum; each is a product of both its environment and the other organisms with which it must compete, avoid or depend on. In most cases, the organisms that make up a given ecosystem fall into one of several, well-established categories. The energy in the food chain all originates from the sun and every bit of living tissue on the planet is eaten by something else in the food chain. Nothing is wasted except heat, which is lost due to inefficiencies at each level of the system.

The green plants of any terrestrial ecosystem form the foundation for the local food chain. They capture the sun's energy and turn it into sugars through the process of photosynthesis. Ecologists call such green plants producers, because they produce the food that feeds the entire ecosystem.

Herbivores, such as Russian tortoises, are called primary consumers, because they feed directly on producers. Those animals that hunt Russian tortoises and other primary consumers are called secondary or tertiary consumers – most people know them as predators.

Scavengers are another form of secondary predator. They eat dead or dying consumers. Eventually organisms called decomposers – primarily bacteria, fungi and invertebrates – break down the remaining bits of organisms that no other creature eats. In this way, they recycle the nutrients from their food back into the food chain, so that other plants can use these resources to perpetuate the cycle.

b) Russian Tortoise Feeding Ecology

Grasses are the most abundant plant types in the Russian tortoise's range. Volga fescue (*Festuca valesiaca*) and Bulbous bluegrass (*Poa bulbosa*) are two common species to the area. Additionally, the area is home to a wide variety of weeds, herbs and succulents. Because of the short growing season and low

22

annual rainfall, few trees exist. However, walnut trees (*Juglans regia*) dot the area. Additionally, the area is home to many pistachio shrubs (*Pistacia vera*) and juniper bushes (*Juniperus turkestanica*).

While only a few studies of their natural diet have been conducted, they have generated interesting – and often counterintuitive - data. Older literature referred to Russian tortoises as generalist grazers that primarily subsisted on grass in the wild. However, current research indicates that Russian tortoises are selective eaters that consume a relatively narrow range of plants in their native habitats.

Despite the opportunity to consume a wide variety of plant species, over 90 percent of their diet is composed of nine different plant genera and species, according to a 2003 study, published in "Ecography." (Fre´de´ric Lagarde, 2003) Contrary to popular thought, the tortoises did not appear to consume grass; instead, they preferred small herbs and weeds. In many cases, the tortoises appeared to be very selective about the parts of the plants they consumed. For example, most Russian tortoises only consumed the flowers of poppy plants (Papaveraceae) and forsook the leaves, but a few did consume leaves as well as the flowers. (Fre´de´ric Lagarde, 2003)

Perhaps most interestingly, Russian tortoises appear to consume some plants that are known to be toxic to mammals. For example, the flowering weed *Papaver pavoninum* is highly toxic to sheep and cattle, yet the tortoises eat it readily and without apparent ill effects. Some scientists have suggested that these plants may serve to help reduce the parasite population in the gut of the tortoises.

Regardless of their reason for their peculiar dietary choices, it serves them well. The combination of their avoidance of grass and fondness for plants that are toxic to mammals helps them to avoid competition with the horses, antelopes and deer, which eat the grasses. As grass is relatively low in calories, these animals must eat large quantities of grass to power their active, "warm-blooded" lifestyle. Eating this much food requires a lot of time, and accordingly, much of the active time of such ungulates is devoted to feeding.

By contrast, Russian tortoises consume much more calorie-rich food sources and are able to survive while devoting only a small percentage of their time to feeding. On average, Russian tortoises spend less than 15 minutes of each day foraging for food. When combined with the fact that this feeding period only lasts for about three months, it is remarkable that these tortoises nourish themselves so easily. (Fre´de´ric Lagarde, 2003)

c) Predators of Russian Tortoises

Few studies exist documenting the predators of Russian tortoises. Well protected by their shells, Russian tortoises have relatively few predators as adults. Young tortoises are undoubtedly killed more often than the adults are, as even small predators can cope with their relatively thin shells. Nevertheless, adults are not invincible, and they probably fall prey to animals such as Corsac foxes (*Vulpes corsac*), which share portions of the tortoise's range. Additionally, wolves (*Canis lupus*), steppe eagles (*Aquila nipalensis*) and Persian leopards (*Panthera pardus saxicolor*) may consume the occasional, unlucky tortoise. Rural humans may also consume the tortoises from time to time.

d) Other Interspecific Interactions

Russia tortoises often take over and modify the discarded burrows of marmots and rabbits. Whether initially constructed by rabbits, rodents or tortoises, the burrows often serve as habitats for other small creatures as well. Spiders, insects and small lizards sometimes use the burrows for shelter.

5. Behavior and Social Structure

Just as the habitat, climate and ecological framework of the region have influenced the morphological evolution of turtles; these factors have also affected the evolution of the tortoises' behavior, social structure and reproductive strategy. Specifically, these factors have caused Russian tortoises to evolve well-developed burrowing behaviors and highly seasonal activity patterns. Russian tortoises rely on these burrows heavily, using them to brumate (the reptilian equivalent to hibernation) to avoid winter temperatures and aestivate to avoid the scorching summer sun. Additionally, Russian tortoises use them as retreats that shield them from predators and the nighttime chill of the steppe.

Most Russian tortoise burrows in the wild are about 3 to 6 feet (2 meters) long. They are often dug into a hillside or directly underneath a large rock, and these burrows may penetrate as far as 6 feet (2 meters) below ground level. They usually feature an enlarged chamber at the terminus, which allows them to turn around more easily.

The sand and dirt of these habitats becomes nearly as hard as concrete as the dry season progresses, and accordingly, the tortoises must often wait until the spring rains arrive to extricate themselves from their tunnels. Russian tortoises have little time to waste; once the brief, active season arrives, they must consume a year's worth of food in about three or four months.

Like most tortoises, Russian tortoises are diurnal. In the morning, they exit their burrows and begin basking in the sun and foraging. If the midday temperatures climb too high, they will retreat to their burrows, possibly returning to forage in the late afternoon. During the peak of summer, some tortoises approach a crepuscular (active at sunrise and sunset) activity pattern.

Russian tortoises subsist primarily on the clumped vegetation in their barren habitats, so they do not have to travel far to find food. In the wild, Russian tortoises often live in densely populated areas. Their burrows can be extremely close to each other in areas of exceptional habitat, and their density may exceed 1800 turtles per square kilometer. Animals are frequently observed sharing burrows.

The adults exit their over-winter homes with the onset of the rains in March or April. They begin feeding and searching for mates almost immediately. The males often bob their heads and engage in assertive postures to show their vigor. During the breeding period, males may engage in combat, attempting to bite or flip each other. Usually, the subordinate animal flees, ending the combat before serious harm befalls either animal.

Females usually flee a male's initial advances, prompting the male to initiate a sequence of dramatic head bobs, and bite the female's legs and face. This causes the female to stop fleeing and retreat into her shell, which allows the male to mount her. Fertilization may follow a single mating, although pairs sometimes mate more than once in a season. Males will mate with as many females as possible.

Because female Russian tortoises are constrained by small body size, they cannot produce very many eggs at a time. Usually, Russian tortoises produce three to five eggs, although occasional clutches may contain as few as one egg or as many as nine. Several weeks after mating, females begin excavating egg chambers 3 to 5 inches (8 to 13 centimeters) deep, using their rear legs.

Once the females have deposited their clutch of eggs, they will cover them back up. Russian tortoises often tamp down the soil and camouflage the egg chamber very well. Sometimes, females deposit a second (and sometimes third) clutch of eggs, several weeks after the first.

Russian tortoises do not provide care of any kind to their offspring; once the eggs are deposited and buried, the next generation is on its own. The young hatch two to three months later, depending on the temperatures. The warmer the eggs are, the quicker they develop. Sometimes the hatchlings remain in the nests throughout the winter, and demerge in the spring.

After the end of the breeding and egg-laying season, adults consume as many calories as possible to survive the long winter, but their activity patterns begin to slow. Some of the tortoises aestivate (a dormant state that occurs during warm and dry weather) from June to August, as the summer heat bakes the land. After they awake in August, they will try to eat as much as they can before the winter sets in. Some scientists and keepers have observed Russian tortoises consuming small sticks and branches in the fall, but the function of this remains unclear. By mid-October, most of the tortoises have burrowed into the earth and begun brumating. They will sleep soundly until the rains arrive in March or April, when they will emerge and begin the process anew.

Chapter 2: Russian Tortoises as Pets

1. The Pros and Cons of Russian Tortoises as Pets (Considerations for Prospective Keepers)

Russian tortoises are one of the most popular turtles among reptile enthusiasts, and for good reason! While no animal is the perfect pet for all people and all situations, Russian tortoises are well suited for captivity.

- They remain relatively small throughout their lives, which makes them more manageable than many other pet reptiles.
- Russian tortoises are almost exclusively herbivorous, which makes feeding them simple, inexpensive and stress-free.
- They are docile and endearing little critters that are a blast to watch, and they are fun companions for walks around the backyard. Many Russian tortoises even learn to eat from their owners' fingers.

Nevertheless, there are a few problems with keeping Russian tortoises as pets, though most of these problems are common to all reptiles.

- Many reptiles can carry salmonella bacteria, which can infect humans. While proper hygiene can reduce the likelihood of this drastically, it remains a possibility.
- Wild-caught Russian tortoises may carry additional pathogens, including bacteria, fungi, protozoa, viruses or parasitic worms. Like salmonella, some of these have zoonotic potential.
- While they can be maintained indoors, it is far better to house Russian tortoises outdoors.
- Russian tortoises require a minimum of 8 square feet (.75 meters) of space per individual, and preferably much more.

28

This is often more space than some keepers are willing to devote to a pet.

- Like all pets, Russian tortoises require resources to maintain. Owners must be willing to bear the expense of the costs related to their food, caging, heating, lighting and veterinary needs.
- Adding a Russian tortoise to the family is a long-term commitment. Russian tortoises can live for at least 50 years, and potentially much, much longer. Contrary to what far too many new reptile keepers believe, the local zoo will not want your tortoise when you grow tired of it. It can be extremely challenging to find a new, appropriate home for an unwanted tortoise.

2. Keeper Responsibilities

When compared with dogs and cats, Russian tortoises are relatively low-maintenance pets. However, they do require daily care and it is important that keepers understand their needs at the outset. Caring for any animal is a great responsibility and a true privilege.

You will need to perform tasks such as visual inspections, water changes and spot cleanings every day. You must also check to be sure that the lighting and heating fixtures are working properly and that the temperatures in the habitat are correct. You will have to pick up feces and urates – if you do not like the idea of this, do not buy a tortoise. While many of the necessary tasks are not fun, you can perform all daily tasks in about 10 minutes if you do so with efficiency and purpose. This is less time than it takes to walk a pet dog once.

In addition to daily tasks, you will have other periodic tasks, such as breaking down the cage and scrubbing it out, taking your tortoise to the vet, purchasing vegetables regularly and changing the light bulbs every six to 12 months.

Think ahead. Many who begin with good intentions ultimately find that they are not willing to allocate the proper time, effort and resources into caring for their critter. Be sure that you can spare 10 minutes per day and a few Saturday afternoons per year to care for your pet properly before you purchase one.

Do not forget to consider the length of this commitment either. Consider where you will be living 10, 20 or 50 years into the future. Do you plan to move, marry, divorce or have children? Could your boss transfer you across the country tomorrow? Your tortoise may out-live you; to whom will you bequeath him?

You must have answers for these questions, or at the very least, the attitude that your tortoise deserves quality care, despite the circumstances in your life. Accordingly, if you decide to become a turtle-parent you must make the necessary sacrifices as they arise and ensure that your tortoise is always healthy and has a high quality of life.

3. Costs

a) Typical Costs

As with any pet, keeping a Russian tortoise costs money. In addition to the acquisition of the pet, owners must have the financial means for obtaining a habitat, as well as the lighting, heating and monitoring equipment necessary. Keepers must also supply their pet with food, water, supplements and veterinary care as necessary. In most cases, you can expect the habitat and associated items to cost at least three times the purchase price of the tortoise.

See the chart below to gain an understanding of the typical costs associated with Russian tortoises. All of the prices listed are estimates; you may find different prices depending on your geographic area.

Do not forget to consider the ongoing costs associated with pet ownership. One cost that many fail to consider is the increase in utility costs that sometimes accompanies animal ownership. Keepers from cold climates, who house their tortoise indoors, suffer the largest increases.

Startup Costs

Item	Estimated Cost
The Tortoise	$50 to $100+ (£30 to £60)
The Habitat	$50 to $500 (£30 to £295)
Heating Equipment	$50 to $100 (£30 to £60)
Lighting Equipment	$50 to $300 (£30 to £177)
Thermometers	$20 to $100 (£11 to £60)
Substrate	$20 to $50 (£11 to £30)
Hides, Cage Props	$20 to $50 (£11 to £30)
Food and Water Dishes	$20 (£11)
Miscellaneous Items	$50 (£30)
Total Upfront Costs	**$330 to $1250 (£194 to £738)**

Perpetual Costs

Item	Annual Cost
Food	$250 to $500 (£147 to £295)
Increased Utility Bills	> $120 (£70)
Veterinary Bills	$100+ (£60+)
Replacement UVB bulbs	$50 to $200 (£30 to £118)
Miscellaneous	$50 to $200 (£30 to £118)
Total Annual Costs	**$500 - $1100 (£295 to £649)**

b) Practical Cost Saving Measures

Over the years, keepers have devised a number of ways to reduce the costs associated with owning tortoises. Most require the keeper trade labor or time for reduced cost, so such measures should not be considered magic bullets.

While it is only logical for keepers to try to reduce their costs, it is important to understand that cost is only one factor in the selection of any item, technique or protocol. Do not make husbandry decisions based solely on price. There are, however, a few things that can be done to cut costs:

- **Growing your own vegetables**
  Many plants grow well directly in your tortoise's habitat and require very little care. However, you may find that your tortoise consumes the plants faster than they can regenerate. If this is the case, it may be beneficial to grow many different plants in the enclosure. Protect one of the plants from your tortoise by placing an open-topped cylinder around the plant. After the plant has recovered from the tortoise's feeding activities for a few days or weeks, remove the barrier and protect another plant. You can also grow vegetables for your tortoise in a separate garden and offer them to your pet at feeding time.

- **Save Kitchen Scraps**
  Many of the vegetable scraps that you would normally discard or compost are excellent tortoise food. Save carrot tops, radish tops, apple peels and the stalks of greens from your kitchen and use them to supplement your tortoise's food. Ensure that kitchen scraps are not contaminated with salt, fats or sugars.

- **Pet Health Insurance**
  Veterinarian expenses can add up to a large portion of your total pet budget. One way to help offset these high costs is to secure pet health insurance. Though not yet available in all areas or for all pets, some companies do offer health plans for pet reptiles. Once enrolled in such a policy, you will pay monthly premiums that will reduce the costs associated with most services.

- **Search Flea Markets and Garage Sales**
  You can find items such as plastic storage boxes, bowls, food dishes and light fixtures at garage sales. If you can find a second-hand store, garage sale or flea market in a rural area, you may be able to obtain livestock troughs and tubs at discounted prices.

- **Shop Hardware Stores Rather Than Pet Shops**
  While some items, such as UV producing light bulbs and mineral supplements, are only available through pet stores and retailers, most of the other items necessary for designing your tortoise's habitat are available – and less expensive – at hardware stores, home improvement stores and other "big-box" retailers. Reflector domes for heat lamps and light fixtures can be found in the lighting or electrical section, while prefabricated pond liners and indoor-outdoor thermometers are usually in the garden section. Many garden sections also have a variety of pots, pans and planters that can be helpful for hiding spots and water dishes. The home storage sections of such retailers often have a wide variety of plastic storage boxes that can be used for transportation tubs, hiding boxes or soaking containers.

- **Playing to Your Strengths**
  Each owner, tortoise and set of circumstances is unique. Do not be afraid to look for innovative ways to solve a problem. Keepers skilled in carpentry may be able to shave down the costs necessary to construct the habitat, while keepers with landscaping experience may save money by housing their pet outdoors, which alleviates the need for heating and lighting fixtures entirely. Keepers who are savvy and patient shoppers may find subtle ways to save money on virtually everything they buy – adding up to significant total savings.

4. Myths and Misunderstandings

Unfortunately, there are many myths and misunderstandings about Russian tortoises and reptile-keeping in general. Some myths represent outdated thinking or techniques, while other myths and misunderstandings reflect the desires of keepers, rather than the reality of the situation.

Myth: *Russian tortoises will only grow to the size of their enclosure, and then they stop growing entirely.*

Fact: Despite the popularity of this myth, healthy tortoises do not stop growing until they reach their final size. Keeping a turtle in a small cage is an inhumane practice that will only lead to a stressed, sick animal.

Myth: *Russian tortoises are reptiles, so they are not capable of suffering or feeling pain.*

Fact: While it is important to avoid anthropomorphizing, or projecting human emotions and motivations to non-human entities, reptiles – including Russian tortoises – feel pain. There is no doubt that they can experience pain and seek to avoid it. While it is impossible to know exactly what a tortoise thinks, there is no reason to believe that they do not suffer similarly to other animals, when injured, ill or depressed.

Myth: *All you have to feed a Russian tortoise is lettuce.*

Fact: No single vegetable will provide for all of the nutritional needs of Russian tortoises. In truth, iceberg lettuce is not even a good *component* of Russian tortoise diets. Russian tortoises need a variety of high calcium, high fiber foods, including wild leaves, weeds, flowers and store-bought vegetables.

Myth: *Russian tortoises can be allowed to roam about unsupervised.*

Fact: Russian tortoises may get themselves into trouble if allowed to roam unsupervised. Even if allowed freedom inside a home, they may chew electrical wires, topple furniture, foul carpets or stain wood floors. If you can design a "tortoise proof" area, and ensure that it does not contain any items that may harm the tortoise, it is acceptable to allow the turtles freedom within a confined area. Leaving a Russian tortoise unsupervised outdoors courts disaster. Your tortoise may be attacked by predators, stolen, hit by a car or it may simply vanish into the local habitat.

Myth: *Russian tortoises are adapted to temperature extremes, so it is not necessary to use a thermometer or monitor the cage temperatures.*

Fact: Russian tortoises have evolved a wide array of adaptations that allow them to survive where few other tortoises can. However, much of the way they do this is by becoming inactive when temperatures are not conducive to activity. Russian tortoises still require temperatures within a fairly narrow range, and as the keeper, you must monitor the habitat temperatures often to ensure the health and well being of your pet.

Myth: *My Russian tortoise likes to be held so he can feel the warmth of my hands.*

Fact: In truth, your Russian tortoise may tolerate being held, but it probably does not "like" it. This myth springs from the notion that because reptiles are "cold blooded," and they must derive their heat from external sources, they enjoy warmth at all times. In truth, while tortoises are ectothermic or "cold blooded," they are most comfortable within a given range of temperatures. This temperature varies with the season and over the course of the day, but averages between 70 and 85 degrees Fahrenheit (21 to 29 degrees Celsius) – your hands are actually a bit warm for the animals.

Myth: *Turtles never bite because they do not have teeth.*

Fact: While it is true that turtles and tortoises lack teeth, their beaks are often strong, hard and sharp. Turtles of about three to four inches in size can easily break human skin with a bite. While some species, such as Russian tortoises, are known for their docile nature, nothing precludes them from biting. To be clear: Russian tortoises are not likely to bite their keepers, but as a keeper, you must understand that it is a possibility.

Myth: *Russian tortoises are good pets for young children.*

Fact: While many turtles make wonderful pets for adults, teenagers and families, they require more care than a young child can provide. The age at which a child is capable of caring for a turtle will vary, but children should be about ten years of age before they are allowed to care for their own turtle. Parents must exercise prudent judgment and make a sound assessment of their child's capabilities and maturity. Children will certainly enjoy pet tortoises, but they must be cared for by someone with adequate maturity. Additionally, it is important to consider the potential for young children contracting salmonella and other pathogens from the family pet.

Myth: *You should carve your initials in an inconspicuous place on your tortoise's shell so that you can identify it if it is ever stolen or lost.*

Fact: Contrary to popular belief, turtles and tortoises do have nerves and blood vessels in their shells. While the outermost layers of keratin lack nerve endings, they can still feel stimuli (including pain) through their shells. Consider that human fingernails – which are also composed of keratin – can most certainly feel stimuli and pain.

You should never cut, carve or drill into your tortoise's shell. In the past, because people often believed that tortoises could not feel their shell, they performed a range of horrific "procedures" on living turtles. One particularly gruesome example was the drilling of a hole through a turtle's shell so that it could be tied to a stake. It is terrible to imagine the pain such turtles would have felt, but it was probably similar to the pain a human would feel if they had a bone or tooth drilled with no anesthesia.

Every so often, a wild turtle is found with a date or person's initials carved in its shell. While this does provide useful data for scientists, it came from a practice that no self-respecting scientist would condone.

Myth: *If you get tired of a turtle, it is easy to find a new home for it. The zoo will surely want your pet; after all, you are giving it to them free of charge! If that doesn't work, you can always just release it into the wild.*

Fact: Acquiring a pet turtle is a very big commitment. Most turtles are long-lived animals, and Russian tortoises have very long lives. They reach at least 40 to 50 years of age in the wild, and they may live much longer than that in captivity. Even if you purchase a wild-caught animal that is already 30 years old, you may have to care for it for 10 or 20 more years.

If you ever decide that your tortoise no longer fits your family or lifestyle, you may have a tough time finding a suitable home for it. You can attempt to sell the animal, but this is illegal in some places, and often requires a permit or license to do legally.

Zoos and pet stores will be reticent to accept your pet – even at no charge – because they cannot be sure that your pet does not have an illness that could spread through their collections. A zoo may have to spend hundreds or thousands of dollars for the care, housing and veterinary care to accept your pet Russian tortoise, and such things are not taken lightly. While Russian tortoises are very neat animals, and they are worthy ambassadors for turtles, they are not rare or especially sought after by such institutions.

Some people consider releasing the tortoise into the wild if no other accommodations can be made, but such acts are destructive, often illegal and usually a death sentence for the tortoise. Russian tortoises are not adapted to the habitats of North America or Western Europe. They will have very little chance of surviving, and even if they do, they will never reproduce.

Even if you live in the tortoise's natural range, captive animals should never be released into the wild, as they can spread pathogens that may wipe out a native population. You will likely have to solicit the help of a rescue group or shelter devoted to reptiles in finding a new home for an unwanted tortoise.

Chapter 3: Captive Care

1. What You Need

To care for a Russian tortoise, you will need a variety of items:

- Some type of enclosure, tub or pen
- A suitable substrate
- Visual barriers and hiding places
- Heating Devices
- Light fixtures and full-spectrum bulbs
- Water and food dishes
- Miscellaneous containers for food, supplies and for transporting your tortoise
- Digital indoor-outdoor thermometer
- Non-contact infrared thermometer
- Misting Bottle (optional)
- Digital scale
- Pens and a notebook or a computer for recording pertinent information (sizes, important dates, etc.)

2. The Enclosure

The first thing to consider when designing any habitat or husbandry protocol is the enclosure. The enclosure is what makes your animal a "captive" as opposed to "wild." Over the years, keepers have successfully employed many different types of enclosures for housing Russian tortoises. While few authorities agree on the best type of enclosure for these little turtles, most agree on a set of important criteria that every cage or habitat must have or provide:

- The enclosure must be secure and prevent the escape of the captives. Likewise, the cage must prevent unauthorized animals (especially juvenile *Homo sapiens*) from gaining access to the cage.
- The enclosure must have no sharp edges or other features that may injure the animal.
- The enclosure must accommodate the necessary heating and lighting fixtures, as well as be easy to service and maintain.
- The enclosure must be large enough to provide the turtle or turtles with enough room to engage in daily activities, receive sufficient mental stimulation and allow sufficient exercise.

At the outset, the first thing that you must decide is whether you plan to use an indoor enclosure or an outdoor enclosure. While outdoor maintenance is generally preferred for this species, it is not always possible, and many keepers have successfully kept this species indoors over extended periods of time.

a) Outdoor Caging

There are a variety of reasons why outdoor habitats are well suited for tortoises in general and Russian tortoises specifically. Almost all tortoises benefit from basking in the unfiltered sunlight of outdoor enclosures and the larger amount of space they usually afford. Additionally, by keeping them outside, you do not have to purchase expensive lighting systems. Russian tortoises specifically benefit from the numerous wild weeds and plants that often grow right in their cage.

However, outdoor maintenance does have a few drawbacks. Outdoor maintenance is not appropriate for all climates. While Russian tortoises are the most northerly ranging tortoise species in the world, they must have adequate temperatures so that they can metabolize their food, have enough energy to forage and stave off illness.

Russian tortoises can often be maintained outdoors in temperate climates as long as they are allowed to burrow sufficiently deep in the winter or they are brought indoors during the cold months. While Russian tortoises will adapt to climates that are not ideal, your local climate must be relatively similar to that which they experience in the wild.

Russian tortoises have evolved to brumate throughout a very long winter, become active during the short spring, aestivate during dry summers and become active again in the fall, shortly before beginning their annual slumber and starting the process over again.

While keepers living in Norway or British Columbia may not be able to maintain their Russian tortoises outdoors because it is too cold, keepers in Miami may not be able to keep them outdoors because it is too hot. In order to maintain Russian tortoises outdoors, your local climate must satisfy the following conditions:

- The ambient daily temperatures must reach the mid-80s Fahrenheit (26 to 30 degrees Celsius) for several hours per day, for at least five months of the year.
- The sunlight should be strong enough to produce basking spots with surface temperatures of at least 100 degrees Fahrenheit (37 degrees Celsius) for at least two or three hours per day.
- The climate cannot have excessive rain or consistently high humidity.
- Russian tortoises benefit from cool nights, and they will not thrive in areas with constantly warm nights – especially if the humidity level stays high.

If your local climate is not warm enough, additional heating elements can be added to the habitat.

If you do not live in an area with a suitable climate for consistent outdoor maintenance, you may be able to utilize outdoor caging for part of the year. If this is not feasible, it is still very beneficial to take your tortoise outside for regular "walks", during which the tortoise can bask in natural sunlight.

In addition to the local climate, several other criteria must be met in order to successfully maintain tortoises outdoors.

- Pesticides, herbicides, fertilizers and other chemicals must not be used in proximity to the habitat. Because groundwater can transport such chemicals, it is important that the habitat be buffered on all sides by several feet (meters) of chemical-free land.
- The area must be free of predators or the habitat must be able to exclude them completely. Potential predators of Russian tortoises include foxes, raccoons, hawks, coyotes and domestic pets.
- The habitat must be installed in an area that is convenient to maintain, yet is located away from areas with high foot-traffic.

Outdoor cages vary in design, as most are custom built for the location. However, they all feature some type of walls, which create the enclosed area. Outdoor turtle habitats often resemble scaled-down versions of livestock pens. Several different materials can be used to construct the walls of the pen.

- Concrete blocks are sturdy, relatively inexpensive and easy to work with (although they are heavy). However, concrete blocks do not look very attractive, and without reinforcing them, they can topple. Furthermore, it can be challenging to attach a roof to the top of the blocks.
- Corrugated plastic panels are lightweight, easy to work with and most animals cannot climb them. However, to be rigid enough, they must be attached to some sort of frame.
- Poured concrete walls are the best possible option, although constructing pens made of such walls is laborious and challenging. However, if you have the expertise, skill and finances to utilize poured concrete walls, they are unsurpassed in terms of utility, stability and aesthetics.
- Chain link fencing, chicken wire and similar materials are not appropriate for the pen walls. In addition to allowing some predators (such as rats) to enter the habitat, Russian tortoises may climb the material or become entangled in it, causing injury.

- Wood can be used to construct the walls, but it will need to be replaced as it rots or covered in an animal-safe sealant.

Regardless of the material used, the walls for a tortoise pen must be at least 16 to 20 inches (40 to 50 centimeters) in height. In general, the higher the walls, the safer the turtles will be, but wall height will reduce the amount of sunlight that shines into the habitat, when the sun is at a low angle. This may be a problem for keepers living at extreme latitudes.

One of the great benefits that outdoor cages provide in contrast to indoor cages is that it is usually easier to provide large accommodations for the tortoises. While it is possible to keep Russian tortoises indoors in about 8 square feet of space (.75 square meters), it is highly desirable to provide much more space than this.

Strive for cages with 40 to 50 square feet (3.5 to 4.5 square meters) of space for up to three turtles. Larger groups necessitate even more space.

On top of the cage, it is usually desirable to place some type of cover. If the walls are smooth and adequately tall (at least six feet or two meters high), then most predators will be excluded. However, this does nothing to stop hawks, vultures, owls and other predator birds from snacking on the turtles. Additionally, raccoons or opossums may climb into the cage from an overhanging tree or structure.

Be sure to allow the natural, unfiltered sunlight to bathe part of the pen, therefore glass, plastic and opaque materials are not good choices for the lid of an outdoor habitat.

While not appropriate for the cage walls, chain link fence, chicken wire and hardware cloth are good materials for the top of an outdoor habitat. They will require some type of frame to remain in place. The lid will have to be removable unless the cage is tall enough to permit you to walk into it from the side.

Another great benefit of outdoor habitats is that they allow a deep substrate. This is especially valuable for Russian tortoises, which routinely dig burrows in the wild. The challenge for the keeper is providing a suitable quantity and quality of substrate, while preventing the captive from tunneling out of the cage or undermining cage props or walls.

The best substrates for Russian tortoises approximate the substrates of their natural habitat. Usually, a mixture of one part sand to one part coconut fiber produces a light, well-drained mix that permits burrowing. Top soil or naturally occurring soil may be used as well, but it must drain quickly after rain. Russian tortoises will not thrive in enclosures that feature poorly drained substrates. The substrate should not be 100 percent sand either. Sand, by itself, does not hold a burrow well and may cause excessive amounts of dust.

Russian tortoises dig as far as 6 feet (2 meters) below the surface in their natural habitat. While they may also do so in captivity, it is rare for them to dig this deeply. Generally, by ensuring that the walls penetrate 18 to 24 (45 to 60 cm) inches below ground level, you can be reasonably sure that your tortoise will not escape. However, further protection can be had by attaching a 12-inch (25-centimeter) length of chicken wire or hardware cloth to the bottom of each wall panel. Place the chicken wire in the hole (which may need widening) so that it extends directly from the base of the wall to the inside of the pen. This way, if your tortoise digs down past the bottom of the wall, it will run into the hardware cloth, thus blocking his attempts at tunneling to freedom.

Always be sure that outdoor habitats feature many different microclimates. A large, flat, gravelly area that receives full morning sun makes a great basking spot for Russian tortoises. However, they also need places with deep shade to escape from the sun during the middle of the day. Furthermore, they need a place that allows them to burrow deeply as a retreat from the heat, and to access the cool, damp air of such tunnels.

b) Indoor Caging

Despite the appeal of outdoor caging, many people opt to keep their tortoises indoors. Indoor maintenance is possible, but the endeavor is often more difficult to execute as the keeper must replicate the Sun, and space constraints are often more severe indoors.

If you have access to a basement or garage, it is possible to construct a pen for the tortoises, much as outdoor pens are constructed. Stacked cinder blocks or framed panels make suitable walls, and substrate can be placed on a liner covering the floor. For such pens, you can suspend the lights with chains attached to the ceiling. If the area is free of pets and children, no lids are necessary.

Indoor pens designed in this manner avoid one of the key challenges of indoor cages: limited cage space. Given an average sized basement or garage, 50 square feet (4.5 square meters) devoted to the turtles may only account for five percent of the total space.

If you do not have access to a place suitable for an indoor pen, you will need some type of container or cage to use for the habitat. Some containers work better than others do, and you will have to decide which type of container works best for your needs.

- Commercially produced, plastic reptile terrariums often work well, feature useful design elements (such as built-in light shrouds) and limit the work necessary to the hobbyist. However, only the largest sizes are appropriate for the maintenance of Russian tortoises. Cages of adequate size will generally cost $300 or more. Some commercially produced cages lack adequate ventilation.
- Glass aquariums are inappropriate for Russian tortoises. Cages of the necessary size are difficult to find locally, incredibly expensive, unmanageably heavy and fragile. Additionally, such cages generally lack sufficient ventilation for these turtles.

- Commercially produced tortoise tubs or tables are a good solution for young turtles; older turtles may require larger accommodations than such products offer. If suitably large tubs or tables are used, these cages are among the best possible options, as they are designed explicitly for turtles.
- Troughs, large tubs or prefabricated pool liners can be used as the base of your Russian tortoise habitat. Prefabricated pond liners are a cost-effective choice for the amount of size they provide, but they often come in irregular shapes. Large cattle troughs, stock tanks and home storage containers work well if they can be found in large enough sizes and appropriate configurations.

The majority of keepers elect to use a trough or large storage box to maintain their captives. This is often the most economical solution, but it is also a technically sound approach.

Troughs can be made of plastic or galvanized metal as long as they are designed to hold water for stock animals. Plastic containers are usually designed with more gradually sloping sides, while the sidewalls of metal troughs are usually vertical. Troughs must have at least 8 square feet (.75 square meters) of space per inhabitant, but it is better to provide much, much more space. Consider that the recommendation for outdoor Russian tortoises is about 50 square feet (4.5 square meters) of space. In all cases, provide your tortoise with as much room as possible. In addition to providing room for exercise, it is easier to generate numerous microclimates in large cages.

While tubs and stock tanks are relatively lightweight when empty, they will become much less mobile when filled with several inches of substrate, heating devices and light fixtures. Accordingly, it can be advantageous to construct a wooden frame with casters or wheels to hold the trough. This will allow you to move it much more easily when the need most assuredly arises, such as when an object falls behind the trough.

It may be necessary to construct frames or lids to hold light fixtures or attach lids if necessary. Tortoises will rarely escape from such cages, but ill-intentioned pets or children can access the tortoises easily, if no lid is used.

Trough-like containers can be constructed from sealed wood or plastic panels. While difficult to construct and design for those not familiar with such work, it allows a great deal of flexibility for adapting the container to the room. There is no reason that the container must be square, rectangular or round.

When constructing a container, consider designing it in such a way that allows you to break down the cage annually for disinfection and repair. For example, utilize bolts and nuts, which are easy to remove, rather than nails or wood screws in construction of the enclosure.

3. Keeping Multiple Animals in the Same Habitat

Often, keepers prefer keeping more than one animal in the same habitat. While this requires careful thought, planning and execution on the part of the keeper, it is possible in some cases. However, beginners often underestimate the increased workload that multiple animals generate.

Because Russian tortoises live in such an unusual habitat and are so uniquely adapted to it, few other species would thrive in similar conditions. Accordingly, Russian tortoises should not be housed with other species. In addition to their differing husbandry requirements, animals from different geographic areas may harbor pathogens that are harmless to them, but may be dangerous to other species that lack such adaptations. This phenomenon is well documented among human explores, who often transmitted diseases to the native peoples of far off lands.

Additionally, it is possible that the interactions among the different species will cause the occupants stress. While not especially timid, Russian tortoises may become intimidated if forced to cohabitate with large species, such as African spurred tortoises. While the other "Mediterranean" tortoises may have a

46

roughly similar size and hail from somewhat similar climates, they should not be housed together either. It is possible that these close relatives will interbreed, producing hybrid offspring. Such offspring may be infertile or have undesirable characteristics. Such chimeras are difficult for breeders to sell or even give away to other keepers. Additionally, if the hybrid offspring strongly resemble one of the parent species, they can be mistaken or misrepresented as being a true member of the species. This can cause problems for breeders and keepers of the species, who must start to question the identity of animals in the marketplace.

Many breeders and keepers house Russian tortoises in small groups. While generally acceptable, the process requires more work and forethought than commonly thought. Rather than simply acquiring a group of tortoises and placing them together in a cage, it is important that you consider the following issues:

- The tortoises must have all passed through individual quarantine periods and be free of pathogens before they are housed together. This can be a problem for a keeper who purchases several animals at the same time and then must scramble to devise as many individual habitats. While quarantine cages need not be as large as the long-term home for the animals, they must still be large enough to allow the animals to thermoregulate and get enough exercise.
- Males will engage in combat during the breeding season, which can lead to serious injuries. Accordingly, the best strategy is to keep one male with several females.
- While you need not double the size of the enclosure for every tortoise you add to the colony, the total area must be large enough for all of the animals to create their own burrows and have enough room to exercise.
- Not all Russian tortoises will cohabitate amicably. For reasons that often escape the eyes of their human keepers, some tortoises will fight routinely. This phenomenon is not limited

to males; females will occasionally exhibit antagonistic behaviors towards other females.

- Russian tortoises exhibit morphological variations throughout their range. While it can be difficult to obtain geographical information about a given tortoise, every effort should be made to assemble colonies that hail from the same area. Do not assume that all of the tortoises a retailer carries are from the same area.

- Always observe new additions carefully for several weeks to ensure they are cohabitating well with the others in the cage. While the tortoises may all get along initially, the social dynamics of the colony may change over time.

4. Lighting

While some reptiles do not require special lighting of any kind, Russian tortoises may become seriously ill if they are not provided with the appropriate type of lighting. Learning how to provide the proper lighting for Russian tortoises is sometimes an arduous task for beginners, but it is very important to the long-term health of your pet that you do so. To understand the type of light your tortoise needs and how to acquire the right type, you must first understand a little bit about light.

Light is a type of energy called electromagnetic radiation and it travels in waves (light also travels as particles, but that is not important for this discussion). These waves may differ in amplitude, which correlates to the vertical distance between consecutive wave crests and troughs, frequency, which correlates with the number of crests per unit of time, and wavelength. Wavelength is the distance from one crest to the next, or one trough to the next. Wavelength and frequency are inversely proportional, meaning that as the wavelength increases, the frequency decreases. It is more common for reptile keepers to discuss wavelengths rather than frequencies.

The sun produces energy (light) with a very wide range of constituent wavelengths. Some of these wavelengths fall within a range called the visible spectrum; humans can detect these rays with their eyes. Such waves have wavelengths between about 390 and 700 nanometers. Rays with wavelengths longer or shorter than these limits are broken into their own groups and given different names.

Those rays with around 390 nanometer wavelengths or less are called ultraviolet rays or UV rays. UV rays are broken down into three different categories, just as the different colors correspond with different wavelengths of visible light. UVA rays have wavelengths between 315 to 400 nanometers, while UVB rays have wavelengths between 280 and 315 nanometers while UVC rays have wavelengths between 100 and 280 nanometers. Rays with wavelengths of less than 280 nanometers are called x-rays and gamma rays. While at the other end of the visible spectrum, infrared rays have wavelengths longer than 700 nanometers, while microwaves and radio waves are even longer.

UVA rays are important for food recognition, appetite, activity and eliciting natural behaviors. UVB rays are necessary for herbivorous reptiles (and some omnivorous reptiles) to produce vitamin D3. Without this vitamin, reptiles cannot properly metabolize their calcium.

The light that comes from the sun and light bulbs is composed of a combination of wavelengths, which create the uniform white light that you perceive. This combination of wavelengths varies slightly from one light source to the next. The sun produces very balanced white light, while "economy" incandescent bulbs produce relatively fewer blue rays and yield a yellow-looking light. High-quality bulbs designed for reptiles often produce very balanced, white light. The degree to which light causes objects to look as they would under sunlight is called the Color Rendering Index, or CRI. Sunlight has a CRI of 100, while quality bulbs have CRIs of 80 to 90; by contrast, a typical incandescent bulb has a CRI of 40 to 50

Another important characteristic of light that relates to tortoises is luminosity, or the brightness of light. Measured in units called Lux, luminosity is an important consideration for your lighting system. While you cannot possibly replicate the intensity of the sun's light, it is desirable in most circumstances to ensure the habitat is lit as well as is reasonably possible. For example, in the tropics, the sunlight intensity averages around 100,000 Lux at midday; by comparison, the lights in a typical family living room only produce about 50 Lux.

Without bright enough lights, Russian tortoises may become lethargic, depressed or exhibit hibernating behaviors. Dim lighting may inhibit feeding and cause the turtle to become stressed and ill. Russian tortoises hail from wide-open habitats; during the summer, the sun is very bright.

To summarize, Russian tortoises require:

- Light of relatively high intensity
- Light that is comprised of a significant amount of UVA and UVB radiation
- Light with a high color-rendering index

Now that you know what Russian tortoises require, you can go about designing the lighting system for the habitat. Ultraviolet radiation is the limiting factor for proper lighting, so it makes sense to begin by examining the types of bulbs that produce UV radiation.

The only commercially produced bulbs that produce significant amounts of UVA and UVB and suitable for a tortoise habitat are linear fluorescent light bulbs, compact fluorescent light bulbs and mercury vapor bulbs. While lighting and heating are separate needs, and not all light bulbs produce significant amounts of heat, and not all heating devices produce light, some of the most effective light bulbs on the market also produce heat.

Neither type of fluorescent bulb produces significant amounts of heat, but mercury vapor bulbs produce a lot of heat and serve a dual function. In many cases, keepers elect to use both types of lights – a mercury vapor bulb for a warm basking site with high levels of UV radiation and fluorescent bulbs to light the rest of the cage without raising the temperature. You can also use fluorescent bulbs to provide the requisite UV radiation and use a regular incandescent bulb to generate the basking spot.

Fluorescent bulbs have a much longer history of use than mercury vapor bulbs, which makes some keepers more comfortable using them. However, many models only produce moderate amounts of UVB radiation. While some mercury vapor bulbs produce significant quantities of UVB, some question the wisdom of producing more UV radiation than the animal receives in the wild. Additionally, mercury vapor bulbs are much too powerful to use in small habitats, and they are more expensive initially.

Most fluorescent bulbs must be placed within 12 inches of the basking surface, while some mercury vapor bulbs should be placed further away from the basking surface – be sure to read the manufacturer's instructions before use. Be sure that the bulbs you purchase specifically state the amount of UVB radiation they produce; this figure is expressed as a percentage, for example 7% UVB. Regardless of the type of bulb used, it will require replacement every six to 12 months.

However, ultraviolet radiation is only one of the characteristics that tortoise keepers must consider. The light bulbs used must also produce a sunlight-like spectrum. Fortunately, most high-quality light bulbs that produce significant amounts of UVA and UVB radiation also feature a high color-rendering index. The higher the CRI, the better, but any bulbs with a CRI of 90 or above will work well. If you are having trouble deciding between two otherwise evenly matched bulbs, select the one with the higher CRI value.

Brightness is the final, and easiest, consideration for the keeper to address. While no one yet knows what the ideal luminosity for a Russian tortoise's cage is, keepers should strive to create very brightly lit enclosures. Sometimes, a single mercury vapor bulb will fail to properly illuminate the enclosure, while two mercury vapor bulbs make the habitat much too hot. It may be necessary to use a combination of linear or compact fluorescent light bulbs along with mercury vapor bulbs to raise the luminosity to a desired level. To err on the side of caution, install high quality, UVA- and UVB-producing bulbs with a high CRI value over two-thirds of the cage so that most of the cage is well-lit, but your tortoise can still retreat to shade if he/she desires.

Connect the lights to an electric timer to keep the length of the day and night consistent. For most pets, it is appropriate to keep the lights on for 12 hours; however, if the plan is to breed the tortoise, it is best to follow a natural annual variation. For example, the lights may be on for 10 hours per day in the winter, 11 hours per day in the spring and fall and 12 hours per day in the summer.

5. Heating

Russian tortoises require supplemental heating when kept indoors. The best way to supply this heat is with incandescent bulbs or ceramic heat emitters, installed in reflector domes. This way, the lights can be suspended above the cage to replicate the sun. If necessary, you can also use heat pads or heat tape underneath the habitat to raise the temperature slightly. However, this will tend to dry out the substrate and can be a fire hazard if the heating devices are not installed properly. Hot rocks, heated perches or other cage props with enclosed heating elements are not appropriate for Russian tortoises.

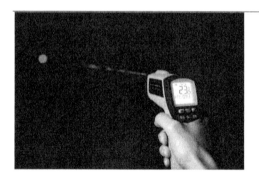

A non-contact infrared thermometer allows you to measure surface temperatures from a distance.

a) Ambient Temperatures and Surface Temperatures

It is important to distinguish between surface temperatures and ambient temperatures. Surface temperatures are best determined by using a non-contact, infrared thermometer. Measure ambient or air temperatures by using a digital, indoor-outdoor thermometer with a remote sensing probe. A Russian tortoise may sit comfortably on a rock with a surface temperature of 100 degrees Fahrenheit (37 degrees Celsius) or more, but if kept in a cage with 100-degree ambient temperatures, it will likely die. The self-adhesive, low-cost thermometers commonly sold in pet stores are not appropriate for monitoring your pet's habitat. Non-contact thermometers are available from specialty electronics stores, medical supply companies and some retail reptile establishments. Indoor-outdoor thermometers are available at pet stores and home improvement stores. You will need one type of each thermometer to care for your new pet.

b) Thermal Gradients

As "cold-blooded" animals, the internal body temperature of Russian tortoises varies over time. Unlike humans who adjust their temperature by sweating when too hot or shivering when too cold, most reptiles have few physiological mechanisms to adjust their temperature. If they need to warm up, they must move into the sun, and if they are too warm, they must retreat to the shade or down into a burrow. Because the natural world has many different microclimates that tortoises can exploit, they are usually able to keep themselves comfortable. The process by which reptiles adjust their temperature behaviorally (by moving to places with different temperatures) is called thermoregulation.

In captivity, it is important to allow your tortoise to thermoregulate as he would in the wild. Ideally, your tortoise should have access to a wide range of temperatures. The best way to accomplish this is with a thermal gradient, meaning that the temperatures in his habitat slowly transition from relatively cool at one side of the cage to relatively warm at the other. To establish a thermal gradient, place the primary heating sources at one end of the cage, rather than in the middle of the cage.

Adjust the heating device until the ambient temperatures under the basking spot are about 90 degrees Fahrenheit (32 degrees Celsius). The surface temperature of the substrate or rock below the basking spot should remain under 125 degrees Fahrenheit (51 degrees Celsius). If in doubt, be sure that you can rest your hand comfortably on the substrate; it can be quite warm, but should not be hot enough to burn.

c) Adjusting the Cage Temperatures
You can adjust the basking spot temperature in a number of ways. You can:

- Change the wattage of the bulb. For example, if a 100-watt bulb is creating a basking spot that is too warm, exchange it for a 75-watt bulb.
- Increase or decrease the distance between the lamp and the basking spot. With flood-style lamps, this will also cause the heat to spread out over a greater area or contract into a tighter area, either of which may or may not be desirable.
- Add an additional heat source, such as an under tank heating pad or a second basking lamp. Under tank heating pads are not appropriate for providing the primary source of heat, but they can be helpful when trying to raise the basking spot's temperature by 5 to 10 degrees Fahrenheit (5 degrees Celsius).
- Install a dimmer switch or rheostat to reduce the amount of heat reaching the basking spot.

- Some keepers have success raising the temperature of their
  enclosure by including massive objects into the cage, which
  increases the thermal mass of the habitat. In other words, by
  placing a large rock, brick or sealed jug of water in the cage, it
  will absorb and slowly re-radiate the heat into the habitat. Do
  not use an open container of water, as it will raise the
  humidity.

Once the basking spot is the correct temperature, with 90-degree
Fahrenheit (32 degrees Celsius) ambient temperatures and sub-
125 degree Fahrenheit (51 degrees Celsius) surface temperatures,
begin measuring the temperatures just outside of the basking area.
In other words, if the basking spot is on the left side of the cage,
start checking the temperatures slightly to the right of the basking
spot.

Test the temperatures all the way to the far end of the cage -- the
ambient temperature should drop slowly with increasing distance
from the heat source. Ideally, the temperature at the cool end of
the cage will be in the low-70s Fahrenheit (low-20s Celsius). By
strategically arranging the props in the cage, you can create even
cooler spots by blocking the light and creating "shade."

If your home is unusually cool, you may need to provide more
heat to the habitat to keep the temperatures at the cool end of the
cage at 68 degrees Fahrenheit (20 degrees Celsius) or warmer.
You can do this with additional basking lamps or heating pads.
Another alternative is to insulate the habitat; but be careful that
the temperatures at the warm side of the cage remain appropriate.
If you are having trouble keeping the habitat warm enough and
you use a screened lid, consider switching to a partially vented lid
so that less warm air will escape. You could also simply cover
part of the screen with a pane of glass or piece of plastic.

More often, keepers struggle to keep the temperatures at the cool
end of the cage sufficiently low. This is a more challenging
problem to fix, but success is attainable with patience. Using spot-
bulbs rather than floodlights is the simplest solution. Sometimes,
switching to two low-wattage heat lamps, rather than one high-

wattage lamp helps to reduce the "bleeding" of the lamp's warmth and contain it on one side.

At night, Russian tortoises appreciate a temperature drop down into the mid-60s Fahrenheit (17 to 20 degrees Celsius). If it is not possible to get their temperature that low, make every effort to reduce the nighttime temperatures as much as possible. You must turn off all heat sources that use visible light at night, but if the temperatures drop too low, you can leave heating pads or lamps with ceramic heat elements turned on. Practically speaking, the tortoises are usually more comfortable with cool nighttime temperatures than their keepers are, making this a rare problem for indoor-housed Russian tortoises.

6. Substrates

Substrate choice is particularly important for Russian tortoises, as burrowing is one of their most important behaviors. The substrate must yield easily enough that the tortoises can dig into it, yet it must retain its structural integrity enough to permit the construction of stable tunnels. Unlike some other tortoises that may thrive with hide boxes instead of burrowing opportunities, Russian tortoises require a substrate that allows burrowing.

Many different hobbyists and breeders swear by a given recipe for making the perfect Russian tortoise substrate. As long as such recipes contain no toxic or harmful types of soil, do not produce excess dust and allow the tortoises to burrow, they should all be acceptable. Most such recipes feature varying amounts of play sand and either coconut fiber or organic topsoil. The sand helps to prevent the substrate from holding too much moisture and ensures adequate drainage, while the coconut fiber or soil has enough moisture and the proper type of structure to maintain burrows.

Russian tortoises will spend a considerable amount of time digging, which makes substrate selection crucial.

It is a good idea to sift any substrates before placing them in your tortoise's pen to prevent including harmful items that may have made their way into the substrate, such as nails, sharp sticks or trash. Provide at least 16 inches (40 centimeters) of soil, but it is preferable to provide 24 inches (60 centimeters) of depth or more. Tamp the soil down firmly before placing the tortoises in their cage.

7. Cage Décor and Furniture

In general, Russian tortoises do not require many items in their cage. While good climbers by turtle standards, Russian tortoises do not require climbing opportunities or elaborate decorations. One thing that all tortoise habitats must include is hiding spaces. Hiding spaces can take a number of forms, and they all have their pros and cons. A few commonly used items include:

- Cardboard boxes make excellent hides, but they must be discarded or recycled when soiled. They are not very aesthetically pleasing, but this is not a problem for the tortoise.
- Lengths of plastic pipe or tubing can be used, but they must be large enough to permit the tortoise to turn around and exit the tube. Rough up the inside of the tube with sandpaper to

allow the tortoise to gain traction. Piping can be buried into the substrate to replicate burrows.

- Some keepers bury clay pots on their sides to create small hiding spaces for their turtles.
- Rocks can be stacked in such a way as to create tunnels and other hiding spaces, but they must be cemented together to prevent collapses. Additionally, the base must rest directly on the floor of the habitat (as opposed to the substrate) to prevent the turtle from digging underneath the rocks and causing them to fall.
- Cork bark can be stacked into a variety of hides. Cork bark is extremely light, so it will not harm the tortoise in the event of a collapse, but it can be difficult to clean and it is quite expensive to purchase.
- Commercially produced hide boxes are easy to clean and require no customization.
- Inverted cat litter boxes and similar plastic containers work well as hides if a door is cut into one of the sides.

Regardless of the type of hide chosen, it must be dark and fit the tortoise somewhat snuggly – ideally, the ceiling of the hide should barely touch the top of the tortoise's shell. Each tortoise should have at least one hiding spot, but two or three per animal is even better.

In addition to hiding spots, it does not hurt to add several visual barriers to the cage, such as rocks or hills. This can be especially helpful when keeping more than one tortoise in a cage. It also contributes to your tortoise's well being, creating mental stimulation.

8. Cage Maintenance

The hobbyist's job is not only to create a good habitat but to maintain it as well. Once you have designed and set up a quality habitat for your Russian tortoise and placed your beloved pet inside the immaculate enclosure, it will immediately begin destroying it. Your tortoise will begin defecating and producing urates, tracking food all over the enclosure and rearranging cage props with its digging activities. As the keeper, you must address this daily wear and tear and ensure that your tortoise's enclosure remains clean and in good order.

There are several different categories of maintenance that must be completed. Some tasks must be performed daily, while other types of maintenance or care must be completed about once a month. Additionally, some in-depth maintenance duties must be performed about once a year.

a) Daily Tasks
- Visually inspect the tortoise and look for any signs of illness or disease.
- Wash, rinse and refill the water dish.
- Wash and rinse the food dish, offer food (some keepers only choose to feed every other day).
- Spot clean the enclosure, removing all feces, urates, shed scutes and other types of debris.
- Ensure that the lighting and heating devices are working properly.

b) Monthly Tasks
- Weigh the tortoise and record the results.
- Soak your tortoise in an inch or two of lukewarm water (some keepers perform this task weekly).
- Clean the walls of the enclosure with a veterinarian-approved disinfectant or 5 to 10 percent bleach solution. Be sure to get all of the cage's corners, and push back the substrate so that you can clean the wall-floor edge.
- Freshen the substrate as necessary. Check to ensure that the moisture level is appropriate and that it smells fresh. Replace any fouled substrate.
- Sterilize water bowls and food dishes by soaking them in a 5 to 10 percent bleach solution for at least one hour. Allow the food dish and water bowl to air dry for at least 24 hours before returning them to the cage.

c) Annual Tasks

- Replace the full-spectrum lights (some bulbs must be replaced every six months – check the bulb manufacturer's recommendations)
- Break down indoor cages, remove all substrate, clean all surfaces and refill the habitat with fresh substrate
- Visit the veterinarian for a checkup if the tortoise has not been for a visit since the last year.
- Replace or clean porous cage props, such as cork bark, branches or hollow logs.

d) Cleaning Techniques and Products

Use a gentle dish soap and hot water to clean water and food dishes. Always be sure that the dishes have been rinsed off thoroughly and no soap residue remains. For cage surfaces, use a veterinarian-approved disinfectant such as chlorhexidine. If this is not possible, add a squirt of dish soap to a 5 to 10 percent bleach solution in a spray bottle, and use this to clean cage surfaces. Use paper towels or a soft scrub brush to clean cage surfaces, and be sure to wash the brush or discard the paper towels after use.

e) During Maintenance

While maintaining your tortoise's habitat, it is best to remove him and place him in a temporary habitat to keep him from being injured or inadvertently sprayed with a cleaning solution. This is one of the reasons that you always want to have a plastic container for temporarily containing your tortoise. By removing him from the cage and placing him in the temporary plastic habitat, he will stay safe and be out of your way.

Plastic storage boxes are the best option for a temporary holding cage. Such cages need not be large, as they will not hold your tortoise for very long. Russian tortoises are comfortable temporarily in shoe-box-sized plastic boxes. If you keep more than one tortoise in the habitat, you can keep them together in their temporary box as well. However, you may need to opt for a slightly larger box. For two or three turtles, a sweater- or blanket-box works well.

You can use transparent or opaque plastic boxes – each has benefits and drawbacks. Clever keepers elect to have both on hand in order to be prepared for all circumstances. For routine use, such as when you are cleaning the tortoise's primary habitat, a transparent box is preferred. It will allow you to observe and monitor the tortoise while you are tending the cage. This is a definite benefit, but there are times when you may not want your tortoise to see through the container. For example, if you must take your tortoise on a long car trip, or carry him through a busy mall to get to the veterinarian's office, an opaque box will prevent the tortoise from seeing all of that activity, which will keep its stress level low.

Drill or burn a few small holes in the lid of the container to provide some airflow. Alternatively, you can cut out portions of the plastic lid and replace it with window screen.

Just like kids tracking mud on the kitchen floor after they have been playing outside, Russian tortoises will track debris from their cage into the temporary box. Additionally, they may defecate or deposit urates while inside, so be sure to clean the temporary cage after each use.

Some keepers like to soak their tortoises as a matter of routine while tending their cage. This is an excellent practice, which helps to ensure that your pet is well hydrated at all times. Other keepers only soak their tortoise periodically; instead, they place their tortoises in a dry, plastic tub while tending their cage.

Chapter 4: Annual Cycles and Brumation (Hibernation)

When reptiles undergo a drastic reduction in activity and bodily processes to survive the winter, it is called brumation (the reptilian correlate to hibernation). Being from places with such long, cold winters, brumation is an important aspect of Russian tortoise biology. The question is, should captive Russian tortoises be allowed to brumate, or should they be kept at constant year-round conditions.

Allowing a tortoise to brumate is a risky endeavor. Unless you plan to breed your tortoise, it is best to keep him or her active year round. However, some tortoises begin showing signs of stress, such as refusing food or sleeping for increasingly long periods of time, if kept at "summer" conditions all year long.

It is not yet clear if brumation plays a role in the long-term health of tortoises, or if preventing brumation reduces the lifespan of Russian tortoises. However, it appears that the only negative result known is that without brumation, Russian tortoises are unlikely to mate and even less likely to successfully conceive offspring.

If you do not plan to allow your tortoise to brumate, you should keep the environmental conditions of the cage as stable as possible all year. This is easiest with indoor cages, as you have total control of the photoperiod and temperature. If you want to maintain your tortoise outdoors, you will need to bring it inside during the winter. It may even be necessary to bring it inside before fall approaches, and the decreasing amounts of daylight cause your tortoise's body to prepare for brumation.

Part of the reason that brumation is not encouraged for beginners is that Russian tortoises have a narrow band of acceptable temperatures in which they can safely brumate. If the conditions are too cold, the tortoise may fall ill, develop local areas of necrosis or freeze to death. If the brumation temperatures are too high, the tortoises may suffer from excessive bacterial growth or they may waste away as their bodies are not cool enough to reduce their metabolism sufficiently.

Because their bodily functions are not operating at full capacity, Russian tortoises are more susceptible to illness during brumation than when they are active. During brumation, your tortoise will be out of sight for weeks or months at a time, which will prevent you from checking on the status of its health regularly. If the tortoise falls ill shortly after entering brumation, you will have no way of knowing until it comes out of brumation or it does not, and you dig it up yourself. In either case, it may be too late for your pet to recover.

If you do intend to brumate your tortoise, it is imperative that the tortoise is in perfect health. Sick tortoises are not capable of mounting an effective defense against pathogens while brumating. A visit to the veterinarian about one month before the intended start of brumation is a good way to be sure your tortoise is healthy. Discuss your brumation plan with your veterinarian and be sure that he or she believes that your tortoise is healthy enough to survive the process.

It is also important to ensure your tortoise's digestive system is completely empty. If it is not, the food in its gut may decay, making the animal ill. Many Russian tortoises begin refusing food days or weeks before the onset of winter anyway, but to be safe, withhold food for about two weeks prior to brumation. Additionally, it is always a good practice to soak the tortoise a few times before it brumates to ensure it is well hydrated and has an empty digestive tract.

The ideal temperature range for brumating Russian tortoises is about 40 degrees Fahrenheit (4 to 5 degrees Celsius). However, they can safely tolerate temperatures between 35 and 50 degrees Fahrenheit (2 to 10 degrees Celsius).
(http://russiantortoise.net/hibernation_journey.htm, 1997)

This can be accomplished by placing the tortoise in a small box, partially filled with substrate that is kept at an appropriate temperature. It can be difficult to find a place with a suitable temperature; many keepers use basements, garages or modified refrigerators to keep the tortoises in the correct temperature range. It is sometimes difficult to get Russian tortoises to settle in and begin brumating in small containers. Occasionally, they have been known to dig their way out of cardboard boxes while trying to get comfortable. They will not be able to dig their way through plastic boxes, but they still may not settle into such boxes.

Alternatively, you can allow the tortoise to burrow into the ground naturally. Russian tortoises seem to be more willing to brumate in this manner, but the approach carries substantial risks. You must ensure that the burrow does not become damaged or flood in the event of heavy rains. You must also be sure that predators are not able to access your pet while it is relatively defenseless. Rats are especially significant predators of burrowing tortoises in the winter and among the hardest to exclude from an outdoor habitat. However, foxes, domestic dogs, coyotes, raccoons and opossums may also attack dormant tortoises.

If the tortoises are housed outdoors, it is probably best to allow them to emerge from brumation naturally, in their own time. In such cases, the tortoises will likely begin exiting their burrows when the spring rains arrive or the air temperatures begin reaching the high-60s Fahrenheit (18 to 20 degrees Celsius).

By contrast, you can end the brumation of tortoises housed indoors whenever you would like to. While they may brumate for six months or more in their native lands, it is not necessary to allow them to brumate for this long a time period. Usually, a six to eight week brumation period is sufficient to induce mating and eventual egg deposition.

When you decide to end brumation, you can do so relatively abruptly. Raise the temperature of their brumation box over the course of about one week, upon which you can remove the turtle from the box, and place him back in his cage. However, you should not expect the tortoise to spring "right out of bed"; instead, it will likely use its burrow extensively and become active gradually, over the course of about one or two weeks.

You can begin offering food as soon as emerges from brumation, but your pet may not begin eating immediately. If your tortoise begins displaying symptoms of illness or fails to resume eating after two weeks, have your veterinarian examine it. If your tortoise has fallen ill over the course of the winter, it is imperative that you treat it swiftly.

Chapter 5: Food and Supplements

Feeding your Russian tortoise a healthy diet is one of the most important and challenging aspects of its care. There is far more to feeding your pet than tossing a handful of lettuce in the enclosure. You must feed him the right types, amounts and relative proportions of food if your tortoise is to thrive. While experts continue to disagree about the fine details of tortoise diets, most agree on the broad strokes.

Russian tortoises are selective eaters in the wild, and their captive diet must provide foods that are similar to those they seek out in the wild. They primarily subsist on weeds, leaves and flowers, while fruits and other vegetation form a very small component of their diet. Very rarely, they may consume insects or carrion, but they can obtain sufficient protein from their vegetables when fed adequate amounts of food. While some good foods are available from supermarkets and grocery stores, Russian tortoises require a variety of foods that are not available in such places.

1. The Basics of the Diet

Each meal you give your Russian tortoise should consist primarily of low-sugar, high-fiber weeds, leaves or grasses. Once per week, you can provide "treats," such as low-sugar fruits, legumes or seasonally available items. Avoid sugary fruits, offering too many root vegetables and excessive high-protein foods (including legumes). This is not to suggest that your pet will die if it eats a carrot or strawberry occasionally, but such food items often cause intestinal disturbance and can cause parasite blooms.

2. The Importance of Variety

The most important aspect of nutritional health is providing your tortoise with a wide variety of foods. This helps to prevent imbalances and ensures that your pet receives a wide variety of micronutrients. Accordingly, Russian tortoise owners should strive to provide as much variety as possible for their pets.

One good way to ensure that your tortoise gets enough variety is by changing up his food each week or two. For example, while you will always want to feed him a base of dark greens, weeds and grass, you can change which greens, weeds and grass you offer him.

Mulberry leaves are wonderful components of a Russian tortoise's diet.

It is also a good idea to rotate your tortoise's weekly treat as well. One week, you may offer honeydew melon, while you may offer thorn-less cactus pads or strawberries the next.

3. Feeding Frequency and Quantity

Russian tortoises require feedings every day or every other day. If you feed your tortoise daily, provide your pet with as much food as he or she can eat in about 20 minutes; for tortoises fed every other day, allow them to eat for 30 to 40 minutes at each meal. Remove any uneaten food and discard or compost it.

Captive turtles are subject to obesity and other health problems if they are fed too much, fed the wrong type of food or not permitted to exercise sufficiently. Turtles rarely deal with the problem of too much food in the wild, so they are apt to stuff themselves if you allow it. Captive tortoises invariably get less exercise than their wild counterparts do, and they can easily put on excess weight.

To ensure that you feed your tortoise enough food, but not so much that it becomes obese, consider the following tips.

- Use a diet with a high quantity of bulky, low-calorie food, such as grasses and hays.
- In addition to daily or every-other-day feedings, some keepers like to leave some edible – but not delicious – forage in the habitat, such as alfalfa hay. This way, the tortoise always has some food if he is hungry, but will be less likely to indulge in a delicious treat if it is not hungry.
- Weigh your turtle frequently, and adjust the amount of food you provide as the weight dictates. Russian tortoises grow very slowly, but they should demonstrate consistent growth until they are adults. Once they are mature, they may keep growing or simply maintain their weight. If your turtle is losing weight or not growing appropriately for its age, increase the amount of food you are offering. Conversely, if your mature turtle is consistently gaining weight, month after month, you should probably reduce the amount of food offered at each feeding.
- Do not attempt to achieve rapid growth in juveniles by feeding a diet high in protein. This is an unhealthy, unnatural

diet for the animals, and it can lead to kidney and skeletal problems.

4. Important Aspects of Dietary Chemistry

As a tortoise keeper, you must understand some of the important components that are present in vegetables, which can affect your pet's health.

a) Calcium and Phosphorus
Tortoises require a considerable amount of calcium in their diet to build their bones and massive shells. However, simply providing a diet that is high in calcium is not enough. It is also important that the foods you give your tortoise have a good ratio of calcium to phosphorus.

Russian tortoises require both minerals to stay healthy, but phosphorus is not in short supply – it is abundant in most green plants. When phosphorus makes up too much of a diet, it restricts the bioavailability of the calcium. This means that even if there is a lot of calcium in a given food, if there is too much phosphorus in it, the tortoise will not benefit from the calcium.

This can make some foods, such as brussel sprouts and broccoli, which have high levels of phosphorus and therefore a poor calcium to phosphorus ratio, poor choices for tortoise food. Minimally, good foods have a 2:1 calcium to phosphorus ratio. However, in the wild, many plants that wild tortoises prefer have calcium ratios of 5:1 or more.

b) Oxalates, Phytic Acid and Goiterogens
Besides phosphorus, the other compounds found in some plants can reduce their nutritional value. Oxalates or oxalic acids are substances found in many vegetables, such as chard and chives, which function similarly to phosphorus, in that they reduce the bioavailablity of calcium.

Additionally, many legumes are high in a substance called phytic acid, which also inhibits calcium uptake. Plants and vegetables high in any of these three substances should be avoided or fed in extreme moderation.

5. Developing the Menu

Unfortunately, the bulk of a Russian tortoise's diet should be composed of items that are difficult to find in grocery stores. This is because most foods that are appropriate for Russian tortoises are not palatable to people. This can be a challenge for many Russian tortoise keepers, so plan carefully to ensure you have enough food for your pet.

Any grasses, leaves or flowers harvested from the wild must be free of pesticides, herbicides or insectides. Although it is not practical to wash grass, flowers or hay, wash as much of your tortoise's food in cool water before offering it to him.

When keeping tortoises outdoors, it is very easy to grow some of their food inside their cage. Many common spices and herbs such as basil grow well and produce edible blossoms and leaves.

Clover and dandelions often spring up in lawns whether they are desired or not – getting them to grow in a tortoise enclosure is almost an inevitability! Both of these plants, and hundreds of other "weeds" are edible and beneficial components that may grow in your tortoise's pen, providing free, high-quality forage.

6. Good Foods for Russian Tortoises

a) Leaves, Weeds and Flowers
Leaves, weeds and flowers should form as much of a Russian tortoise's diet as possible. Unfortunately, such items are very difficult to come by, and you will likely be forced to harvest such plants from your back yard or some other place.

- Mulberry leaves
- Petunia leaves and flowers
- Dandelion leaves and flowers

- Hibiscus leaves and flowers
- Rose leaves and flowers
- Clover leaves and flowers
- Common sorrel
- Basil
- Prickly pear (with spines removed)
- Blackberry leaves and flowers (remove thorns)
- Squash blossoms

b) Grasses

Grasses do not make up a large portion of the diet of wild Russian tortoises, but grasses are still very high-quality foods that should form a small portion of your pet's menu. Many of the grasses that are common in residential landscapes are edible, palatable and nutritious for tortoises, and include:

- Alfalfa hay
- Timothy hay
- Bermuda grasses
- Fescue grasses
- Rye grasses
- Couch grass
- Buffalo grass
- Kikuyu grass
- Blue Grama grass
- Dallas grass
- Wintergrass
- Bluegrass
- Wheat grass
- Crab grass
- Tall oat grass
- Orchard grass
- Raspberry leaves and flowers (remove thorns)
- Grape leaves

c) Grocery Store Vegetables

The grocery store is the easiest place to acquire food for your tortoise, but most of the foods are not appropriate for your pet. While some of the vegetables in the grocery store, such as endive, cactus pads and collard greens, can serve as regular components of your tortoise's menu, others are only appropriate when offered in moderation. Many of the common vegetables at the grocery store are very high in oxalic acid, phytic acid or phosphorus.

In some cases, farmer's markets and specialty grocery stores may stock vegetables that are more appropriate for Russian tortoises. For example, Greek and Mediterranean grocers often stock grape leaves, which are a great food source for your tortoise (be sure to only purchase fresh, freeze-dried or frozen grape leaves, not the pickled variety that comes packed in brine solution).

- Kale
- Escarole
- Radicchio
- Squash (sparingly)
- Zucchini (sparingly)
- Cucumber (sparingly)
- Parsley (sparingly)
- Collard greens
- Turnip greens
- Radish greens
- Carrot greens
- Cactus pads (thorns removed)
- Banana leaves
- Dill weed (not all tortoises find this palatable)
- Lambs lettuce
- Arugula
- Cress
- Japanese radish greens

d) Fruits

Fruits should only serve as a small part – essentially a very occasional "treat" – for your Russian tortoise. If you prefer, you can avoid fruits entirely, and only feed your pet greens, weeds and grasses. The primary problem with fruits is that they have very high levels of sugar. When this sugar makes its way into the tortoise's digestive system, it often initiates a parasite population explosion, which can cause the tortoise to have intestinal distress.

- Apples (remove cores and seeds)
- Pears
- Blackberries
- Raspberries
- Honeydew Melon
- Cantaloupe
- Mango
- Figs
- Persimmons

7. Toxic Plants

Many wild and domesticated plants may be toxic to Russian tortoises, and as the keeper, you must carefully avoid offering these plants to your pet. Additionally, it is important to inspect any outdoor areas where your tortoise is permitted to graze, to ensure that no toxic plants will be eaten.

There is not much information available regarding plant toxicity as it relates specifically to Russian tortoises or even tortoises in general. Most plants commonly presumed to be toxic are designated as such because they are known to be toxic to dogs, cats, livestock or humans; or because their chemical composition suggests that they may be toxic.

One may wonder how tortoises survive in the wild without keepers to prevent them from eating toxic plants. The most likely explanations are that tortoises have physiologies that make them insusceptible to many plant-based toxins, they specifically avoid toxic plants, or, by virtue of their grazing habits, they avoid consuming effective doses of toxic plants.

 It is also important to note that Russian tortoises have not evolved along the wild and domestic plants that grow in North America or Europe. Whatever the mechanism at work, for keepers of Russian tortoises, it is most prudent to err on the side of caution.

This list is not exhaustive; it only contains some of the most common plants commonly regarded to be toxic. Your local poison control office or veterinarian can provide a comprehensive list of poisonous plants that are common to your area. Never allow your tortoise to consume a plant or vegetable unless you are certain it is safe.

Potentially Toxic Plants for Russian Tortoises:

Common Name	Scientific Name
Amaryllis	*Amaryllis belladonna*
Anemone	*Anemone* sp.
Anthurium	*Anthurium* sp.
Arrowhead Vine	*Syngonium podophyllum*
Asparagus Fern	*Asparagus sprengerii*
Atamasco Lily	*Zephyranthes* sp.
Autumn Crocus	*Colchicum autumnale*
Avocado	*Persea Americana*
Azalea	*Rhododendron sp.*
Baneberry	*Actaea* sp.
Begonia	*Begonia* sp.

Common Name	Scientific Name
Bird of Paradise	*Poinciana gilliesii*
Black Cherry	*Prunus serotina*
Black Locust	*Robinia pseudoacacia*
Black Snakeroot	*Zigadenus* sp.
Bloodroot	*Sanguinaria canadensis*
Boston Ivy	*Parthenocissus tricuspidata*
Boxwood	*Buxus* sp.
Common Name	**Scientific Name**
Buttercup	*Ranunculus* sp.
Butterfly Weed	*Asclepias* sp.
Caladium	*Caladium* sp.
Calla Lily	*Zantedeschia* sp.
Candytuft	*Iberis* sp.
Carolina Jasmine	*Gelsemium sempervirens*
Castor Beans	*Ricinus communis*
Cherry Laurel	*Prunus caroliniana*
Chinaberry	*Melia azedarach*
Christmas Rose	*Helleborus niger*
Clematis	*Clematis* sp.
Cowslip	*Caltha palustris*
Daffodil	*Narcissus* sp.
Delphinium	*Delphinium* sp.

Common Name	Scientific Name
Dumbcane	*Dieffenbachia* sp.
Foxglove	*Digitalis purpurea*
Giant Elephant Ear	*Alocasia* sp.
Gloriosa Lily	*Glonosa superba*
Golden Chain Tree	*Labunum anagryroides*
Common Name	**Scientific Name**
Goldenseal	*Hydrastis canadensis*
Holly	*Ilex* sp.
Horse Chestnut	*Aesculus* sp.
Hyacinth	*Hyacinthus orientalis*
Hydrangeas	*Hydrangea* sp.
Ivy (Common / English)	*Hedera helix*
Irises	*Iris* sp.
Jack-In-The-Pulpit	*Arisaemia triphyllum*
Jerusalem Cherry	*Solanum pseudocapsicum*
Junipers / Red Cedars	*Juniperus* sp.
Lilly of the Nile	*Agapanthus africanus*
Lilly of the Valley	*Convallaria* sp.
Lobelia	*Lobelia* sp.
Lucky Nut	*Thevetia peruviana*
Marijuana	*Cannabis* sp.
Mountain Laurel	*Kalmia latifolia*

Nandina	*Nandinaa domestica*
Nightshades	*Solanum* sp.
Periwinkle	*Vinca minor* and *V. major*
Common Name	**Scientific Name**
Philodendron	*Philodendron* sp.
Pittosporum	*Pittosporum* sp.
Poinsettia	*Euphorbia pulcherrima*
Pothos	*Pothos* sp.
Primrose	*Primula* sp.
Privet	*Ligustrum* sp.
Rosary Bean	*Abrus precatarius*
Schefflera	*Schefflera* sp.
Shasta Daisy	*Chrysanthemum maximum*
Spider Mum	*Chrysanthemum morifolium*
Split Leaf Philodendron	*Monstera deliciosa*
Spring Adonis	*Adonis vernalis*
Strawberry Bush	*Euonymous* sp.
Trumpet Flower	*Solandra* sp.
Umbrella Tree	*Schefflera actinophylla*
Water Hemlock	*Cicuta maculata*
Wisteria	*Wisteria* sp.
Yellow Allamanda	*Allamanda cathartica*

8. Supplements

Despite the best efforts of tortoise keepers to feed their pets a nutritious, well-balanced diet, it is a very hard task to accomplish. To help offset potential deficiencies, many tortoise keepers supplement the diet of their turtles with extra minerals and vitamins.

Usually, such supplements come in powder or liquid form, and they are designed to be mixed in with a tortoise's food or given orally. For obvious reasons, it is easier to mix supplements into your tortoise's food, rather than try to coax him to open his mouth.

Most keepers use two different types of supplement: a multivitamin and a calcium powder. Sometimes, calcium powders are also fortified with vitamin D3 to ensure that the tortoise can properly metabolize the calcium. Vitamins and calcium powder are best kept separate from each other to allow for differential doses.

The proper dosages of vitamins and calcium are poorly understood. If a tortoise receives too much supplementation of either vitamins or calcium it can lead to serious health problems. To be safe, discuss your tortoise's needs with your veterinarian to arrive at a safe dosage schedule. Although hypercalcaemia (too much calcium in the bloodstream) is much rarer than hypocalcaemia (too little calcium in the bloodstream), it is a possibility worth considering when devising a calcium supplementation schedule. While hypocalcaemia causes a number of potential health problems, hypercalcaemia can cause serious health problems as well, including renal failure.

Generally speaking, most tortoise keepers provide vitamin supplements once per week. Calcium supplementation varies based on the age and gender of your tortoise. Young, quickly growing tortoises and reproductively active females require more calcium than adult males do.

When females are producing eggs, they require very high levels of calcium. Without enough, their health may be in danger as well as the health of the developing offspring. To help reduce the chances of a problem, many keepers place cuttlebones in a female's habitat during the breeding season, with the hope that the female will supplement her own diet as necessary. Many tortoises ignore cuttlebones throughout the year, but then consume nearly the entire bone over the course of a day or two, as the time for egg deposition approaches. Cuttlebones have the additional benefit of helping to keep your tortoise's beak from becoming overgrown.

If your tortoise is housed outside, it is unlikely that he is deficient in vitamin D3, so opt for a calcium powder without it. By contrast, even though indoor tortoises should be provided with UVB lighting to help them produce their own vitamin D3, they likely do not produce enough to metabolize all of their calcium.

Chapter 6: Water

To keep a Russian tortoise healthy and happy, you must keep it well hydrated. Unfortunately, much of the conventional wisdom surrounding the issue of water for tortoises from arid habitats is misguided. Many keepers feel that their tortoises get enough water from their food to satisfy their needs; however, this assumption is wrong.

While most vegetable-based foods do contain a lot of water, and Russian tortoises have evolved a number of adaptations to help them conserve water, they still require regular access to fresh drinking water. Russian tortoises are well adapted for living in dry habitats, but they do drink water when they feel parched.

Tortoises that suffer from chronic or long-term dehydration may develop serious health problems. While many organ systems are affected by dehydration, the kidneys perhaps suffer the most. Renal failure is often the ultimate cause of death.

Wild-caught tortoises are usually dehydrated upon arrival in North America or Europe. Because few wholesalers and retailers take the necessary strides to re-hydrate their inventory, most wild-caught Russian tortoises are severely dehydrated by the time they land in the hands of pet owners. Accordingly, pet owners are wise to ensure that their pet is well hydrated at the outset.

Ensuring proper hydration is primarily accomplished by providing your tortoise with the proper food and access to drinking water. For tortoises that are extremely dehydrated, it is also wise to soak them in a small amount of water for brief periods. Some keepers soak their turtles as part of their standard operating procedure.

Most keepers agree that tap water is perfectly acceptable for tortoises. However, the municipal water in different areas has different chemical characteristics. If you find that your tap water is excessively hard (high mineral content), smells strongly of chlorine or contains dissolved metals, consider adding a water filter to your tap or switching to bottled water for your turtles. If you elect to use bottled water, either use purified water or spring water. Do not use distilled water, as the tortoises do require some minerals in their drinking water.

1. Drinking

Keep a low, shallow dish of clean, fresh water in the habitat at all times. Be sure that your tortoise can access the dish and drink from it easily. In general, tortoises prefer low profile dishes, as they will often walk into the water dish before they begin drinking.

A nearly infinite variety of tubs, bowls or dishes may work as a good water bowl. Any number of kitchen products or plant saucers may work, or you can opt for a commercially produced water bowl if you do not feel like being creative.

Stainless steel, plastic, glass or ceramic are common materials from which bowls are made. Ceramic or glass bowls are usually the best products, but they are heavier and more expensive than plastic or stainless steel bowls. While heavy bowls require more effort for the keeper to lift, wash and fill, they are better for tortoises, as they are less likely to flip them over and cause spills.

The size of the water dish will affect the humidity level of the habitat. A large, wide water dish may raise the humidity significantly while a relatively small, narrow water dish will not raise the humidity very much. Use this to your advantage: If your habitat tends to become too dry, a larger water dish will help offset this tendency. Conversely, cages that are perpetually damp may dry out some if the size of the water dish is reduced. In outdoor or open-air habitats, the water dish's influence on the relatively humidity will be insignificant.

Be sure to wash the water dish with mild soap and water every day. Rinse the bowl out thoroughly to ensure that no soap residue remains in the dish. Once per month, soak the dish in a 5 to 10 percent bleach solution for 30 to 60 minutes. Rinse the dish thoroughly and let it air-dry for 24 hours or more before returning it to the habitat. It is a good idea to purchase two water bowls. This way, when you remove one bowl for cleaning, you can swap it out with the spare. Additionally, if one of the water dishes cracks or starts leaking, you do not have to drop everything and go out to purchase a replacement.

2. Soaking

Soaking a tortoise is a great way to ensure that it is fully hydrated. All newly acquired tortoises should be soaked several different times over the course of about one week. You do not have to soak well-acclimated, healthy Russian tortoises regularly, but it is a beneficial practice. Consider soaking your tortoise while you are performing cage maintenance each week; this helps to save time and accomplish two tasks at the same time. Regular soaks will keep your tortoise well hydrated and help keep its feet, tail and plastron cleaner.

To soak a Russian tortoise, fill a smooth, clean plastic storage container (or similar vessel) with a very little bit of lukewarm water. The first few times you soak your tortoise, measure the temperature with the probe from your digital indoor-outdoor thermometer and be sure that it is in the 70s.

The goal is to have enough water to get the bottom quarter of the turtle's body wet – not force him to struggle to keep his head above water. Tortoises drown quite easily, so be sure that the water is not deep enough to drown the inhabitants, should they accidentally flip themselves over in the water. Provide young tortoises with no more than one-half inch of water depth; adults can safely use about two inches of depth.

Soak your tortoise for at least 15 minutes, but no longer than one hour. You will have to monitor your tortoise throughout the duration of the soak to ensure he does not become distressed. Additionally, many tortoises defecate or pass urates while soaking. This is both a benefit and a drawback to soaking tortoises – you will have to deal with the mess your tortoise creates in the soaking container and rinse your pet off afterwards, but you will not have to clean the mess out of the cage.

Always wash the soaking container with soap and water after each use. Let it dry out completely between soakings.

3. Misting

Some reptiles live in areas with naturally high humidity; in captivity, their keepers often mist their enclosure with lukewarm water to raise the humidity or simulate rain. Because they hail from arid climates, misting is not a regular component of Russian tortoise maintenance. While they must be properly hydrated, Russian tortoises will not thrive in damp environments. They are extremely susceptible to moisture-related illnesses, and their habitat should be relatively dry. Nevertheless, there are a few cases in which misting may be appropriate.

Keepers of tropical reptiles often use large, canister-style spray bottles that use compressed air to propel the water. Such tools will work for misting a Russian tortoise's food or habitat, but it is overkill. A small, hand-held spray bottle that costs about one dollar will work perfectly well for the typical needs of a Russian tortoise.

One such example is when you are feeding a dehydrated tortoise. While the vegetables already have a lot of water in them, you can mist them lightly to provide even more water for your pet. Many keepers mist their tortoise's food as a matter of practice. Be sure that the food does not become saturated or slimy; you just want to add a little bit more moisture to the outside. When you need to mist food items, turn the spray nozzle until it produces a coarse spray composed of large droplets of water.

Often, Russian tortoise cages become excessively dry and dusty, thanks to the constant drying action of the heat lamps. If your tortoise's cage becomes too dusty, a light misting may help to clear the air. When this is necessary, adjust the spray bottle so that it discharges the finest mist possible.

Another time when misting may be helpful is during breeding trials. Many captive turtles can be induced to mate by misting them with lukewarm water during the spring and early summer. Be careful not to make the enclosure too wet when misting for this purpose, and be sure that the cage dries out quickly afterwards. Large water droplets will work better than a fine mist for this type of misting.

Chapter 7: Interacting With Your Turtle

Many keepers enjoy spending time with their tortoise, looking at it as more of a "pet" than a "specimen." While your Russian tortoise will never fetch your slippers or learn how to roll over on command, they do interact with their owners more than many reptiles do. The key to all human-tortoise encounters is to appear non-threatening to your tortoise and to establish a history of calm, deliberate interactions. This will allow your pet to relax while in your presence and go about its business naturally.

1. Stress

As humans know well, stress is very taxing. While humans can quickly recover from short-term, minor stresses, long-term stress can lead to serious illness. Russian tortoises react similarly to stress – short-term minor stresses are no problem, but significant or long-term stress can cause serious health decline, reproductive failure or death.

However, the events that cause human stress are different from those that cause tortoises to stress. While humans become stressed from the demands of work and family, Russian tortoises become stressed when dehydrated, malnourished, forced to live in an inappropriate habitat or confronted with potential predators.

To keep your pet healthy and happy, you must limit these sources of stress. Simply providing proper husbandry for your tortoise ensures that it is healthy, well fed and living in an appropriate habitat. However, even with all of these factors under control, your tortoise must still come face to face with a predator every day – you!

While your tortoise will become accustomed to your presence over months or years, and soon view you as the harmless creature that brings it food, this will take time. You can accelerate the process by moving slowly, limiting the turtle's stress and handling it very gently. Teaching your turtle to feed from your hand is a good way to convince them that you mean them no harm.

When planning to spend time with your pet, consider the setting from your tortoise's point of view. Pets, people, loud noises, traffic and other things that are normal for people to cope with are foreign and likely frightening stimuli for your pet. Always keep the surroundings calm to avoid stressing the tortoise. Do not expose your pet to rowdy children or unruly pets; and keep the room you are in quiet and activity-free.

It is important to learn to recognize the signs of stress so that you are alerted to the problem and can take strides to rectify it. Russian tortoises often exhale loudly when startled or stressed – while a relatively subtle hiss indicates a mildly irritated turtle, louder such sounds are indicative of a high stress level. Biting is a very rare behavior for Russian tortoises, and this behavior should be a sign that your tortoise is seriously stressed and should be left alone. Do not confuse an accidental nip from a hungry Russian tortoise as a true "bite," that indicates a stressed animal.

Additionally, Russian tortoises often withdraw into their shell in response to virtually any unexpected stimuli. Whether it is a barking dog, a loud child or a leaf, gently falling from the sky, Russian tortoises are apt to retreat to the safety of their shells immediately. When they realize that the stimulus is not harmful, they will come back out of their shells. If a Russian tortoise pops right back out of its shell when the apparent danger has passed, then it is not likely excessively stressed. By contrast, a tortoise that remains in its shell for long periods of time is probably experiencing serious stress.

Russian tortoises may defecate or urinate when frightened or stressed. However, they are also likely to when drinking, soaking, eating or walking long distances; so, it does not necessarily indicate stress. Some tortoises void their cloacas anytime they are lifted from the ground, no matter how accustomed they become to their keepers.

2. Handling Your Pet

When you need to lift your tortoise, support him completely. The tortoise will feel more secure if he can feel your hands (the "ground" from his point of view) with his or her feet. Be careful though – their claws are not very sharp, but they may be able to cause a minor scratch.

While you can certainly pick up your tortoise to move him from one place to another, or to inspect his health up close, you should not carry him for extended periods of time. In addition to stressing your pet, he or she is likely to urinate or defecate on you if frightened.

If your Russian tortoise does not re-emerge from its shell shortly after a perceived danger has passed, it may be suffering from high levels of stress.

Some tortoises learn to like having their necks or heads scratched. Others learn to eat from their keeper's hands. Some make excellent subjects for photography projects while others prefer to be left alone. Each tortoise has a slightly different personality, and it is incumbent upon the owner to understand the likes and dislikes of the tortoise.

3. Transporting Your Tortoise

If you need to transport your tortoise from his cage to the back yard, your hands will probably suffice. However, when travelling longer distances, such as to the veterinarian or on a field trip for some time in the natural sun, you will need to secure a good transportation container.

Plastic storage boxes work well for Russian tortoises; and they need not be large containers either. Your tortoise will be safer for brief trips if he is in a relatively snug container. A plastic shoe- or sweater-box will work perfectly. If you must take your tortoise on a longer trip – for example if you must move – a slightly larger box would be more appropriate to give him more room to stretch out.

Pad the bottom of the box with some fresh substrate or folded newspaper to provide greater comfort and absorb any liquids that your tortoise may release during the trip. Drill or burn several small holes in the lid of the container to provide ventilation for the tortoise. If the trip is to be long or potentially bumpy, add some crumpled newspaper or cloth towels to the box to keep your pet from being unnecessarily jostled.

There are two schools of thought regarding opaque or transparent boxes. Transparent boxes allow you to observe the tortoise during transport, but they may cause the tortoise more stress, as it can see all of the unusual activity outside the box. Opaque boxes probably keep turtles calmer during transport, but the keeper has to remove the lid to check on their wellbeing. Understand that reptiles and other exotic pets often generate considerable interest when they are brought to public places. If you must travel to or through such places with your pet, do it the favor of using an opaque box to keep a low profile.

4. Outings (aka "Field Trips" or "Turtle Walks")

Field trips are an excellent way to spend time with your tortoise, and it provides the tortoise with some time to bask in natural sunlight and consume some naturally growing forage. Tortoises that are normally housed indoors derive important benefits from such outings, and keepers should make every effort to provide them.

Finding a suitable place to let your tortoise roam about is the first challenge. Your yard is the best choice, as it can be difficult to ensure that chemicals have not been applied to other areas. It is hard to beat a chemical-free yard with lots of sunlight, shade and tasty tidbits tortoises. It is important for the tortoise to have easy access to both sunlight and shade so that he can thermoregulate.

Remember that the chemicals your neighbors use do not stop at the property line. If your neighbors apply herbicides, insecticides or fertilizers to their lawn, it is likely that yours is contaminated as well.

If your yard is not appropriate for walks, you may have trouble finding an acceptable place for your pet to roam. Consider local nature preserves and parks or organic farms, but always obtain permission from the owner before bringing your tortoise to the location. Never take for granted that such places do not use chemical treatments – verify that no harmful chemicals are used on the grounds before allowing your tortoise to walk and feed.

You must keep an eye on your tortoise during such walks, and never leave your pet's side. It only takes a moment for a stray dog or feral cat to attack your turtle. Likewise, tortoises do not understand barriers such as streets, and they may wander into traffic with horrible consequences. Additionally, keepers often fail to comprehend just how quickly a tortoise – even a large one – can disappear into the brush. Do not take your eyes of your tortoise when allowing him or her to get some exercise.

Finally, as when walking your dog, be sure to pick up after your tortoise. Place all excrement in a plastic bag, tie it shut and place it in a trash receptacle. This is especially important for exotic pets, such as Russian tortoises, to ensure that harmful pathogens or intestinal flora are not spread into the environment.

5. Hygiene and the Handler

Your cute little tortoise may harbor pathogens that can make you very sick. While it may be impossible to eliminate any possibility of disease transmission, you can drastically reduce the odds of becoming sick by practicing good hygiene. Additionally, by starting with a captive bred animal, and visiting the veterinarian frequently, you can further reduce the chances of an unpleasant eventuality.

Use the following tips and strategies to help keep you and your family safe from the germs your pet may harbor:

- Always wash your hands after handling tortoises (or any other pets). Use a quality soap and warm water, and wash your hands for at least 45 seconds. Pay special attention to your fingernails.
- If soap and water are not immediately available, you can use a waterless, alcohol-based hand sanitizer to remove many pathogens. However, you will still need to wash your hands with soap and water as soon as possible.
- Never wash cage items in kitchens or bathrooms that are used by people. A utility sink is the best place to wash cage props and tools.
- While you can cut and prepare your tortoise's vegetables in the family kitchen, they should be stored somewhere closer to the tortoise's enclosure, if possible. This will limit the amount of cross contamination that may occur as you travel from the tortoise enclosure to the refrigerator. You can use a small refrigerator to store the vegetables or you can simply prepare fresh food for each feeding.

- During routine soaking time, use a soft-bristled brush to scrub the undersides, tail area and legs of your tortoise. This will help remove feces and other bacteria-laden grime from your tortoise. Be sure to proceed gently, but most tortoises will learn to accept gentle brushing.
- Keep your tortoise's cage as clean as possible. The longer feces, uneaten food and other organic debris sits in a cage, the more bacteria will grow. Perform daily spot cleanings; periodically, break the cage down and clean all surfaces.

Chapter 8: Breeding

Many keepers eventually seek to breed their tortoises. As successful captive propagation helps to offset the number of animals taken from the wild, it is a noble pursuit. Furthermore, as it is one of the most accurate indications that the keeper is providing appropriate husbandry, most keepers with an eye towards breeding take great strides to ensure their pet's health – another admirable trait. However, breeding tortoises is not an activity that should be taken lightly. At best, you will succeed and end up having to provide food, space and care for two to six more Russian tortoises; at worst, your beloved pets could die of reproductive complications.

1. To Breed, or Not to Breed?

Assuming you are successful, you must have a plan for the hatchlings. You may have the resources and desire to keep them yourself, but if you do not, what will you do? While it is true that captive bred Russian tortoises are valuable assets and many people make a living (in part) by breeding them, there is more to selling animals than simply producing hatchlings. Depending on your location, you may have to obtain local, state or federal permits to sell live animals. You may be required to form a licensed business, obtain insurance or move to a commercial location. In addition to all of these costs, you must still market and advertise your offspring, while competing with other breeders who already have a foothold in the market place. Suffice it to say, it can be very difficult to find a customer willing to purchase your animal; it is essentially impossible to generate a profit as a newcomer.

However, you may want to simply give your hatchlings away to other tortoise enthusiasts or be willing to take your lumps and launch your tortoise breeding empire. In such cases, you can begin to consider breeding your Russian tortoises.

2. Distinguishing Males from Females

Even if you do not intend to breed your tortoises, you may still desire to know whether your new pet is a "he" or a "she." Besides, you have to know whether to call your tortoise "Jack" or "Jill"!

Fortunately, Russian tortoises are sexually dimorphic, meaning that males and females have different body shapes. However, these differences are somewhat subtle, and it can take practice to learn to diagnose the differences.

Males are able to right themselves much more easily than females can. This particular animal is a male – note the long tail.

The most visually obvious difference between the two genders is the difference in tail length. Gently flip your tortoise upside down and examine its tail. Males have long tails that extend far beyond the margin of the shell. By contrast, females have very short, nub-like tails that barely extend past the margin of the shell. The female's anus covers most of the ventral side of the tail while the male's anus only covers a small part of the tail. If you have two turtles of different genders, the differences are plainly obvious. In addition to having longer tails than females, the two posterior most ventral scutes on males flare widely, while those of females are smaller and meet at a more acute angle.

Scientists have uncovered several other differences between the genders. However, most of these differences are highly subjective and are of little benefit to the average hobbyist. However, understanding these differences is informative, as it demonstrates how the tortoises have responded to evolutionary trends and pressures. Male and female Russian tortoises are faced with different challenges and they have responded in slightly different ways.

For example, on average, males are lighter (even relative to their shell size), have longer legs and are faster than females. Females have wider shells relative to the males, are built more robustly and take longer to right themselves after being flipped on their backs than males are.

This final tendency reflects the need for males – who engage in combat with other males and are often flipped upside down during the encounters – to be able to flip themselves back over and avoid a certain, helpless death. The fact that females have proportionally wider shells than the males reflects their need to carry eggs.

3. Assembling a Breeding Group

Obviously, you will need at least one male and one female tortoise. However, many breeders obtain much better results by utilizing larger groups of animals. This often makes it difficult to be certain whom the parents of a given clutch were, but it is more likely to produce some eggs.

The task of assembling a breeding group is not easy. Ideally, you would start with captive bred offspring, but you may lack the patience to wait a decade or two for the animals to fully mature. So, you may be forced to work with wild caught animals.

Tortoises should not be involved in breeding trials or climactic cycling protocols unless they are in perfect health. It will usually take several months and several hundred dollars in veterinary expenses to get to the point where you have a group of health tortoises.

Once you have assembled a group of promising, healthy candidates, you must ensure that the individual animals are compatible with each other. Much like with humans, dogs or cats, some individual Russian tortoises simply do not get along. Whenever placing tortoises together, observe them closely for several weeks. Sometimes, aggressive tendencies can arise suddenly, and fighting can ensue.

If two tortoises do not get along, remove one and try again in a few weeks. If this absence does not make them more amicable, refrain from housing those two individuals together.

Unfortunately, as the size of the colony grows, the addition of a single turtle can cause other turtles, who formerly cohabitated well, to fight savagely. Ultimately, assembling a good breeding colony necessitates ample the process of trial-and-error.

While some experienced breeders keep Russian tortoises in large colonies of 20 or more individuals, beginning breeders should keep colonies relatively small in number. Two males and three or four females is a good size for a colony. Watch the males closely for signs of aggression and remove the submissive male from the habitat.

4. Preparations and Pre-Breeding Conditioning

To induce the proper biological conditions for successful breeding, you will have to provide the tortoises with conditions that roughly parallel those that they would face in the wild. This involves altering their temperature levels and photoperiod so that it matches that of the advancing seasons. Most importantly, you must allow them to dig deep tunnels in which they can brumate for the winter.

Tortoises housed outdoors will likely synchronize their bodies with the natural passing of the seasons, particularly if you live in a temperate (as opposed to subtropical) climate. For tortoises housed indoors, the keeper will have to adjust the photoperiod and thermal conditions to mimic seasonal changes.

5. Mating

When it is time to wake the turtles from their slumber, proceed slowly. For the first several days, the tortoises may not eat and may only bask for a short period of time. Allow them to wake at their own rate, and provide food as they begin to show interest. Shortly after becoming active, the males will begin pursuing females. It is also at this time that the males are most likely to engage in combat, so monitor them carefully. Despite their harmless appearance, tortoises can bite each other savagely, causing serious bodily harm to the other animal.

Mating is not always a gentle affair, and the males may bite at the female's heads while trying to get them to accept their advances. They may mate more than one time, but one mating is usually sufficient for fertilization. However, males may attempt to mate with females repeatedly. If this is allowed to go on for an extended time, it can cause the females great stress. The best solutions are to either remove the males for a few weeks until they calm down and then reintroduce them to the communal cage, or incorporate more females in the cage to spread out the stress.

6. Egg Deposition

While the females are holding the developing eggs, they may eat more than usual. They may also seek out sources of calcium, which is in high demand for producing eggshells. Many breeders place a cuttlebone in the cage during the breeding season; if the females are in need of calcium at this time, they will usually consume the cuttlebone.

As the time of egg deposition approaches, you must make a decision. The female will want to dig a small hole in which to deposit her eggs. You can allow the females to deposit their eggs inside the cage and allow nature to take its course, or you can dig up the eggs and incubate them artificially. Egg incubation is something of an art and a science that challenges the best of keepers; often, hobbyists and recreational keepers are best served by simply utilizing "natural incubation" and your tortoise's instincts.

If you plan on incubating the eggs yourself, consider removing the tortoise from her enclosure and placing her in a temporary tub, filled with appropriate substrate. This will allow easier retrieval of the eggs after they have been deposited.

Because Russian tortoises require a substrate that enables tunneling anyway, you can use a similar substrate for a temporary egg-laying tub. The substrate must be sturdy enough that it retains its shape when a burrow is made, yet yielding enough that the tortoise can dig in it. It often helps to dig a small "starter hole" for the tortoise. She will usually take advantage of the work you have already completed.

When ready to deposit the eggs, the female will back into the hole and deposit two to six small eggs. When finished, she will cover the hole and tamp down the substrate very deliberately. Usually, Russian tortoise egg nests are rather well concealed.

7. Postpartum Female Care

Take good care of the female after she has buried her eggs. Give her a gentle bath to remove the excess substrate and any fluids that may be present. Ensure that she has access to plenty of fresh water, food and a warm basking spot. If possible, keep her separated from other turtles for one to two days to allow her to fully recover.

8. Egg Incubation

If you are going to incubate the eggs yourself, begin digging them up immediately. Be very careful as you progress, and stop once you reach the eggs. Slowly uncover the egg mass (they may or may not be stuck together) and clear the dirt away without disturbing the eggs. With a graphite pencil, mark the top of every egg. This way, if the eggs become jostled, you can return them to the proper orientation. Tortoise embryos float up to the top of the egg and attach themselves to the inside of the shell. If the egg is later turned upside down, the hatchling will drown inside the egg.

You will need to place the eggs in a small plastic storage container, filled with damp (not wet) vermiculite. Most breeders use a 1:1 ratio of vermiculite to water by weight for egg incubation media. Place the eggs in the vermiculite so that they are buried about two-thirds of the way to the top of each egg.

Do not attempt to separate the eggs if they are adhered together, simply remove the entire egg clutch from where the female deposited it, and place it in the egg box in the same orientation. Arrange the vermiculite so that it supports the egg mass and prevents it from tipping over. Try to place some vermiculite on top of the eggs, but do not cover any of the eggs completely. The eggs do not need much air – they were buried underground – but they do need some air.

Drill a few very small holes in the top of the box for air exchange. This storage container now keeps the eggs safe and appropriately hydrated, but you must control the temperature as well. This is accomplished by placing this egg box in a larger box with a thermostat-controlled heat source, such as a piece of heat tape or a light bulb.

You can build such an incubator yourself if you are so inclined, or you can purchase a commercially produced unit. Beginners often have their hands full with the process of breeding, and they will benefit from purchasing a commercial unit. The egg container goes inside the incubator for the duration of the process.

Maintaining proper temperatures for Russian tortoise eggs is very important. Not only does it influence the rate at which biological processes happen inside the egg (just as the temperature affects adult tortoises) but incubation temperatures also determine the gender of the baby tortoises.

Unlike humans and many other animals, whose gender is determined genetically, the gender of most chelonians (and some other animals, such as geckos) is determined by the temperature at which the eggs are incubated. This phenomenon is called temperature dependent sex determination, often abbreviated as TDSD or simply TSD.

There are several different models of TDSD, and each produces males and females in different patterns. For example, most chelonians exhibit type IA TDSD. This means that temperatures at the high end of the acceptable range usually produce females, while temperatures at the lower end of the range produce males. By contrast, type IB TDSD produces males at the high end of the range and females at the low end of the acceptable temperature range. Type IB is common in geckos and crocodilians.

Type II TDSD occurs when there are three different temperature ranges: low temperatures, moderate temperatures and high temperatures. In such animals, females are produced at both temperature extremes, while males are produced in the intermediate temperature range.

As a matter of practicality, many turtle breeders opt to set incubation temperatures at the middle of the acceptable range. Such temperatures are most likely to yield viable hatchlings of either sex, and they produce hatchlings of both sexes, which helps from a marketing perspective.

Russian tortoise eggs are best incubated at 88 degrees Fahrenheit (31 degrees Celsius) for a period of about 60 days. This produces hatchlings of both genders, and is well within the tolerances of the eggs. However, individual tortoises, incubators and keepers experience variable results. Some tortoises hatch as early as 56 days, while others take over 75 days to hatch.

If you have decided to allow the eggs to incubate naturally, in the ground, you can do a few things to help ensure that they hatch. The two things that are most likely to ruin the developing eggs are predators and the flooding of the egg chamber. The temperature fluctuations experienced by the eggs are partially mediated by the soil on top of them. This means that temperature swings are not as likely to kill the eggs, but it may accelerate or decelerate their development.

You can help protect the nest from most predators by covering the egg-laying site with a metal grate. Use a grate that covers not only the egg chamber, but also covers 6 to 12 inches (10 to 20 centimeters) of dirt beyond the egg chamber in all directions. Either stake the grate into place or weigh it down to prevent predators from dislodging it.

To protect the eggs from flooding, examine the placement of the egg chamber in the habitat. Look for the path that rainwater will take through the habitat. It is not necessary to protect the egg chamber from short periods of rain, as the soil will likely absorb the water long before it penetrates into the chamber. However, flowing water, such as a channel of runoff water that travels through the habitat, may very well destroy the eggs. If you are concerned about this, use metal, wood or plastic planks to build a dyke system that routes the water around and away from, the eggs.

9. Care of the Hatchlings

When the eggs complete their development, the enclosed turtles will break free using their egg teeth, which will fall off shortly after hatching. Some turtles will seemingly run out of their eggs, eager to take on the world, while others will hatch, but remain inside their egg for days. Some turtles hatch before they absorb the contents of the egg yolk. This is not necessarily a problem, but all efforts should be made to ensure that the structure does not desiccate or become injured until it is absorbed.

Place hatchlings in a warm, quiet container for a few days. Place a very shallow water dish in the container so that they can drink if they desire. More importantly, the water container will raise the humidity of the temporary container, helping to prevent dehydration.

After a day or two in the temporary container, you can move the hatchlings to a habitat set up specifically for them. The habitat should be a scaled-down version of that used for their parents, including appropriate substrate, adequate heating and lighting, fresh water and access to nutritious foods. However, it may take up to two weeks for the hatchlings to begin eating. In the wild, they occasionally remain underground until the spring.

Do not house hatchlings with the adults – though rare, it is possible that a hungry adult would eat a hatchling. Even if they are not predatory, the larger adults may inadvertently injure or intimidate the fragile hatchlings.

Be very careful that water dishes provided to hatchlings are very shallow to prevent the young chelonians from drowning.

Young tortoises are fragile organisms. If you plan on placing the tortoises with another keeper or selling them on the open market, you must wait until they are at least one month of age – six months of age would be even better. The transportation process will stress the young tortoises, as will adjusting to the new sights, sounds and smells of a new home. To give the young turtles the best chance at survival, wait as long as is reasonable before shipping them out.

In some places, you may be legally obligated to keep the tortoises for much, much longer. In the United States, federal law prohibits the sale of any turtle with a shell less than four-inches in length, unless they are sold for scientific or educational purposes. It may take your one-inch-long Russian tortoise hatchlings four years – and maybe even longer – to reach that size.

Chapter 9: Veterinary Care

1. Finding a Good Tortoise Veterinarian

Even though many tortoises live long, trouble free lives, all tortoise keepers must have a reliable reptile-oriented veterinarian that can treat your pet, should it fall ill. Even if your tortoise never gets sick, it may incur an injury that requires veterinary attention.

The best time to find a reliable veterinarian is before you need one. Ideally, you will find a veterinarian qualified to treat your Russian tortoise before you even purchase one. This way, you can take your turtle in for an initial check up on the way home from the breeder or pet store.

Unfortunately, not all veterinarians are qualified to treat tortoises. The biology, husbandry needs and appropriate treatments for tortoises are very different from those of dogs and cats. However, a skilled veterinarian that specializes in reptiles, if not specifically turtles, does exist, and it is important to locate one.

To find such a reptile-oriented veterinarian, you can perform internet searches, look in the back of reptile-related magazines or talk to other tortoise keepers that you meet online or at local reptile societies or clubs. If you have a conventional veterinarian that cares for your dog or cat, he or she may be able to provide a recommendation or referral to a good vet for your tortoise.

In some circumstances, such as keepers who live in rural areas, there may not be any reptile-oriented veterinarian within driving distance. In such cases, it makes sense to contact a reptile-oriented vet who will perform a phone consultation with a conventional veterinarian, who can then treat your pet.

103

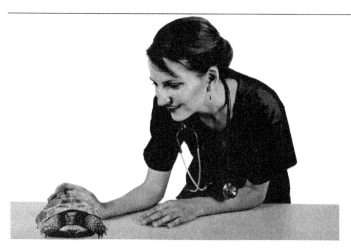

The best time to find a competent turtle veterinarian is before you need one.

2. Common Health Problems and Their Resolutions

While tortoises may incur a wide variety of illnesses, the most common afflictions include respiratory illnesses, infections from pathogens, nutritional problems and traumatic injuries. All of these problems require a veterinarian's assistance to rectify. While infections, parasite issues and nutritional problems can often be avoided with proper husbandry, traumatic injuries can occur under even the best possible care.

a) Respiratory Infections
Many exotic tortoises suffer from respiratory infections in captivity. Sometimes, these infections are the result of opportunistic, ubiquitous bacteria that are able to colonize stressed, poorly kept tortoises. At other times, these infections are spread from one turtle to another, just as the common cold spreads among people. While a tortoise's immune system may successfully eradicate minor infections, some may not be treatable, even with antibiotics and veterinary care.

Symptoms of respiratory infections include:

- Clear, white, yellow or green discharge from the nostrils or mouth
- Labored breathing
- Depression
- Lethargy
- Irritability
- Anorexia
- Increased time spent basking or sleeping in subterranean tunnels

If you observe signs of a respiratory infection, you must act quickly. Firstly, separate the sick tortoise from any cage mates. Secondly, ensure that all of the husbandry parameters of the tortoise's habitat are ideal; the temperature, humidity level and substrate moisture should be tweaked until they are perfect. Thirdly, make an appointment with your veterinarian.

If you have more than one tortoise, always be sure to care for the sick one last. This way, you will help reduce the chances of transmitting communicable pathogens to the others. Additionally, clean all cage tools that are used on sick animals with soap, water and a 5 to 10 percent bleach solution immediately after use.

Your veterinarian will perform a physical examination, review your husbandry practices and take a sample of fluid from your tortoise's nose, mouth or trachea. The veterinarian will then have the sample sent to a laboratory for analysis. The laboratory will usually place the sample in a petri dish with a food source. A few days later, scientists will examine the bacteria, identify it and determine which antibiotics are effective against it.

Sometimes, the veterinarian will prescribe a broad-spectrum antibiotic while the lab work takes place. Once the bacteria's sensitivity has been determined, the veterinarian may change the prescription to a more effective and narrow medication.

While many respiratory infections are bacterial, they can also be caused by fungal or viral problems. These are often more difficult to treat than bacterial problems. No matter what the causative agent is, prompt veterinary attention is required whenever respiratory symptoms appear.

Tortoises can be plagued by infections in other organ systems as well, but they are most common in the respiratory tract.

b) Parasite Issues

Most wild animals have parasites. While these usually cause few serious problems for the animals, parasites can be more serious for captive animals. Wild-caught Russian tortoises almost always have parasite infestations. While captive bred tortoises are less likely to have significant levels of parasites, they should still be monitored regularly, particularly if they cohabitate with other tortoises.

Parasites can cause several different symptoms:

- Anorexia
- Vomiting
- Watery stools
- Weight loss
- Poor growth
- Failure to thrive
- Reproductive problems

Parasites typically live in the intestinal tract of a tortoise, and release eggs that pass with the tortoise's feces. Typically, parasites build up to harmful levels because of three factors: the stress of captivity reduces the tortoise's natural defenses; undersized habitats force the tortoise to have more contact with its own feces; and poor cage hygiene. When kept in a dirty or cramped enclosure, the tortoise can inadvertently ingest parasite eggs, causing their parasite load to grow.

Tortoises can become infected with roundworms, hookworms, pinworms and tapeworms. Additionally, a number of protozoans

106

and other microorganisms are possible parasites. Most are easily eliminated with proper medications and a strict approach to cage cleanliness.

One protozoan that commonly afflicts Russian tortoises is *Hexamita parva*. This parasite lives in the kidneys and urinary tract of Russian tortoises and can be quite damaging. Symptoms of such infection include weight loss and dehydration. If the condition is not rectified soon enough, fatal renal failure can result.

Generally, treating parasite infestations involves administering medication two or more times, and keeping the turtle's habitat immaculately clean until the parasites have been eliminated.

c) Nutritional Problems

Nutritional problems are common for many herbivorous reptiles, especially tortoises. The reasons for these problems are multifaceted, and avoiding them takes a considerable amount of effort on the part of the keeper.

Obesity is very common among captive tortoises, and it is caused by excess caloric intake and insufficient caloric expenditure (exercise). Obesity may cause organ failure, heart problems, lethargy, depression and shortened lifespan.

While the remedy is fairly straight forward – reduce the amount of food you offer and increase the amount of exercise they receive – it can take turtles a long time to lose weight. Always reduce the amount of food offered gradually; never put a tortoise on a starvation diet or withhold food entirely.

You can increase the amount of exercise your tortoise receives in a number of ways. If possible, increase the size of the tortoise's habitat. If this is not possible, or the tortoise already has a large cage but does not use much of it, consider re-arranging the cage props and furniture. This will often encourage the turtle to explore the cage more frequently. Of course, taking your turtle on outings will often peak its curiosity and get it moving.

Nutritional secondary hyperparathyroidism is another common condition that can affect turtles, in which the animal does not have adequate blood-calcium levels to remain healthy. This causes the animal's body to pull calcium from the bones. For tortoises, much of this bone comes from their shell. If left unchecked, this problem – called metabolic bone disease – is invariably fatal.

Nutritional secondary hyperparathyroidism can be caused by not ingesting enough dietary calcium or from a deficiency in vitamin D3, which is crucial for calcium metabolism.

The reason nutritional secondary hyperparathyroidism is more common in herbivores than carnivores is that animal food often contains sufficient vitamin D3 that the predator does not need to produce as much vitamin D3 itself. By contrast, while calcium is often abundant in dark, leafy greens, there is virtually no vitamin D3 in plant tissues. This sets up a situation in which a tortoise may be fed enough calcium, but is unable to use it, as it has a deficiency of vitamin D3. As explained in the chapter on lighting, tortoises produce vitamin D3 when they are exposed to UVB radiation.

Additionally, some minerals, notably phosphorus, reduce the bioavailability of calcium. Ideally, tortoise food should have a 2:1 ratio of calcium to phosphorus.

The most common signs of these conditions are malformed, soft or broken bones. Frequently, this affects an animal's jaws, limbs or their shell.

Very young tortoises have somewhat flexible shells. Do not confuse this with nutritional secondary hyperparathyroidism or metabolic bone disease. This is simply a reflection of the fact that it takes a lot of calcium (and therefore a lot of time) to make a tortoise's shell strong.

If you suspect that your tortoise has nutritional secondary hyperparathyroidism, or is exhibiting symptoms of metabolic bone disease, see your veterinarian immediately.

If caught early, it may be possible to restore a tortoise's health. Your veterinarian will assess your pet's condition and develop a proposed course of treatment. This will invariably include adjusting your husbandry practices to halt further damage; but it may also include providing calcium or vitamin D3 either orally or via injection.

The best way to avoid nutritional problems is to provide your tortoise with the following:

- A diet rich in dark, leafy greens, weeds and grasses
- Provide ample access to natural sunlight
- If access to natural sunlight is not possible, you must employ high-quality lighting that produces ample amounts of UVB. You must also replace the light bulbs regularly.
- Supplement your tortoise's food regularly with a calcium supplement and a vitamin supplement, which is consistent with your veterinarian's recommendation.
- Ensure that your tortoise gets enough exercise and does not become obese.

d) Traumatic Injuries
While often avoidable with the benefit of hindsight, traumatic injuries can occur to even the most careful of keepers. Because tortoises do not vocalize their pain or exhibit outward signs of injury, it is important to inspect your captives daily. Turtles are hardy animals that can survive and overcome profound injuries, but prompt care is not only crucial for raising their odds of surviving, but it is a matter of humane treatment as well. Despite their emotionless faces and lack of the cute, cuddly appearance of dogs or cats, Russian tortoises can feel pain and suffer.

Examples of traumatic injuries include:

- Burns from faulty heating devices
- Lacerations from stray nails or screws in the habitat
- Sharp- or blunt-force trauma wounds from falls or collapsing cage props
- Bites and gnaw wounds from dogs, cats, rats, raccoons and other predators

The proper protocol for dealing with a traumatic injury varies depending on the type of injury involved. In almost all cases, a trip to the veterinarian or pet emergency room is in order. Before leaving the house, try your best to stabilize the animal so that no further harm comes to it and it is able to relax as much as possible. Cover bleeding wounds with a clean cloth or non-stick bandage, keep the turtle in the dark as much as possible and seek medical attention for your pet.

3. Keys to Good Health

As a keeper, you cannot eliminate all potential sources of illness or harm. Accordingly, the wisest course of action is to establish protocols that eliminate the majority of problems and to be prepared when your tortoise inevitably becomes sick or injures itself. By practicing these seven keys to good health, you are very likely to succeed in giving your tortoise a long, healthy life.

1. Begin with a captive bred animal.
2. Have and take advantage of a high quality veterinarian.
3. Provide your tortoise with at least 25 square feet (2.3 square meters) of space; more is better.
4. Be sure your tortoise has a proper thermal environment with access to several different microclimates.
5. House your tortoise outside or take it on frequent excursions so that it can bask in unfiltered sunlight. If housed indoors for any significant length of time, provide high quality, full spectrum lights that produce a significant percentage (> 5 percent) of UVB.

6. Feed your Russian tortoise a wide variety of dark, leafy greens. The greater the variety, the less likely your tortoise will develop nutritional problems.
7. Provide your Russian tortoise with a substrate suitable for digging long tunnels.

Chapter 10: Acquiring a Russian Tortoise

So now that you have decided to acquire a Russian tortoise, where do you get one? There are many different markets to consider, and each has its pros and cons. In general, as with most things in life, you get what you pay for when shopping for Russian tortoises.

Not all Russian tortoises are created equally, and this is an especially important factor for new keepers, who are unlikely to succeed with turtles that are not already in perfect health. Beginners should always seek out captive bred animals if possible; failing that, they should opt for long-term captive animals that have been certified by a veterinarian to be in good health. The worst option for beginners is to purchase freshly imported turtles from wholesalers and resellers. Such animals are common at swap meets and reptile expos.

1. Captive Bred vs. Wild Caught

Russian tortoises reach the pet trade in two primary ways: they are collected from the wild or they hatch in captivity. For pet owners, captive bred animals are superior in every way possible, although breeders may have a need for wild caught animals to increase the diversity in their colony's gene pool. Captive bred animals are healthier, better acclimated to captivity and place no pressure on wild populations. By contrast, wild caught animals are usually loaded with parasites, sick, dehydrated and severely stressed. Wild caught animals are usually less expensive than captive bred animals, but in the case of Russian tortoises, this difference in price is modest. In actuality, the lower price of a wild caught animal is an illusion – once adjusted for the expensive veterinary bills that always accompany wild caught animals, captive bred animals are often more affordable. While dedicated and astute beginners can succeed with wild caught animals, success is much more likely with captive bred animals.

2. Places to Purchase or Adopt Russian Tortoises

a) Breeders

The best place to find a captive bred Russian tortoise is from a tortoise breeder that works with the species. Purchasing a captive produced animal from a reputable breeder is an entirely different experience than any other form of acquisition.

In most cases, breeders are eager to share information and provide support for new keepers. Most dedicated, conscientious breeders are very fond of the animals, and keen to see them thrive in their new home.

Often, by purchasing from a breeder, you can select the animal you want from a wide selection of animals. In virtually all circumstances, the breeder will be able to show you the parents of the animal you like, and he or she may be able to provide you with information specific to the individual you selected, such as food preferences, growth rate and health history.

There are a few drawbacks to purchasing your animal directly from a breeder; they often run out of stock quickly and they often charge more than any other source. While finances are a real factor for hobbyists and no one has infinite funds, the premium paid for acquiring a quality animal directly from the breeder is well worth the expense.

However, being willing to spend the premium price to obtain a Russian tortoise does not guarantee that you will be able to find one. Captive bred stock is always at a premium, and you may have to join a wait list to have the opportunity to buy one.

Breeders can be found in the back of reptile- and pet-oriented magazines and through online searches. You can also inquire with local reptile clubs about local breeders.

b) Pet Stores

Pet stores are probably one of the most common places to purchase a Russian tortoise. Pet stores often have reasonably low prices, but there is a reason for this. Until demonstrated otherwise with robust paperwork and provenance, consider pet store turtles to be wild caught. If a pet store does have true captive bred offspring for sale, they are likely to be priced at about the same level that a breeder would charge. However, they are not worth the same price as the breeder is not likely to offer support and free information to non-customers. Additionally, the animals are likely not provided with the same level of care that they received from the breeder.

However, pet stores are not a bad place to obtain Russian tortoises. In fact, because they often have many different tortoises to choose from and also carry many of the items you will need to maintain the tortoise, sometimes pet stores offer discounts on merchandise upon the purchase of a tortoise.

Additionally, pet stores give patient shoppers the opportunity to observe a given tortoise on multiple occasions before purchasing it. This increases the odds that you will spot any health concerns before purchase. This is particularly true if you are able to watch the tortoise exhibit different behaviors, such as drinking, eating and defecating.

Pet stores often offer health-guarantees for newly purchased pets. Take advantage of this fact by taking any new purchases directly to the veterinarian for an examination. Small problems, such as mild dehydration, may be easily treated with veterinary assistance, allowing you to keep the tortoise. However, if the veterinarian suspects or finds evidence of serious illness, such as a heavy parasite infestation or respiratory infection, return the tortoise to the store and have them refund your money. If the health problem the first turtle had was communicable, avoid purchasing any of the other Russian tortoises that store has in stock; they are likely to be sick as well.

114

Pet stores typically charge between $30 and $75 (£17 to £44) for Russian tortoises. If they carry captive bred specimens, expect them to be priced at $100 (£50) or more.

c) Pet Expos and Swap Meets

Pet Expos and swap meets are becoming increasingly popular in both the United States and Europe. They offer a unique marketplace for acquiring Russian tortoises, but it is wrought with problems.

As often happens at swap meets, animals change hands several times. Accordingly, it can be difficult to impossible to determine the origin of a given animal, sitting on someone's table.

Russian tortoises are usually cheapest at such events. Wild caught individuals may be available for as little as $20 at times. However, as with wild caught animals purchased anywhere else, these animals are unlikely to thrive in the hands of new keepers.

Occasionally, you may find a breeder of Russian tortoises at such an event. Always cast a skeptical eye towards claims of captive bred tortoises; usually, breeders will produce ample evidence of their breeding success without you even asking for it.

Always select a tortoise that appears alert, has clear eyes and no discharge from the nose or mouth.

d) Online Markets

Many online marketplaces exist for purchasing pet reptiles. Essentially, a customer goes to a retailer's website or an online classified website to find an animal. Payment is sent in advance, and the animal is shipped overnight to the purchaser. While the practice of shipping a Russian tortoise in such a way is acceptable if executed correctly, many retailers fail to pack the animals correctly. This can lead to illness or even death. While many retailers offer live-arrival guarantees, it is important to ensure that this is the retailer's written policy. The cost of the shipping is invariably passed on to the consumer, even if it is rolled into the price of the animal.

While such marketplaces allow you to purchase an animal from anywhere in the world, purchasing an animal without seeing it in person is always risky. While professional breeders are unlikely to risk their reputations by sending sick or otherwise flawed animals to customers, many other retailers lack such scruples.

e) Reptile Rescues and Similar Organizations

Unfortunately, many people purchase reptiles impulsively. Such people fail to consider the amount of labor, effort and money that are required to maintain the poor animal, and eventually seek a new home for it. After failing to sell or give away their pet, they turn it over to a reptile rescue or similar organization. Given their long life spans, many tortoises end up in such places. Because they are common pets, many of these tortoises turn out to be Russian tortoises.

These rescues are always keen to place the animals in their care in the hands of responsible, dedicated and compassionate keepers, even beginners. Usually those looking to adopt a tortoise from this type of organization will have to pay a nominal fee and sign a pledge to provide good treatment for the animal.

Rescues and similar organizations are usually very helpful if you have a problem, and they are happy to provide you with a great deal of information.

The drawback to such places is that you do not know the history of the animal in question. It may have been cared for very poorly for an extended period of time. This could shorten its lifespan or force you to pay for very expensive veterinary care.

3. The Quarantine Process

Whenever you acquire a new tortoise, you should treat it as though it is sick (even though you have hopefully purchased a healthy animal from a reliable source). This means that you should quarantine it from all other chelonians until you are certain that it is in good health. If your new pet is the only one you own, then it is in a de facto state of quarantine unless and until you add another cage mate. However, it is possible that you could serve as a vector for disease spread. If, for instance, you handle your tortoise, become contaminated with some pathogen and then go to a nearby pet store, you may spread that pathogen to one of their tortoises if you handle it.

Most authorities recommend a 30 to 90 day quarantine period; however, zoos and other professional institutions often utilize 180-day or longer quarantine periods to be certain that they do not introduce pathogens into established collections. While 180 days may be excessive for the average keeper of a pet tortoise, 30 days may be too short to rule out parasites that lay dormant for an extended period. Of course, if you discover that your tortoise is suffering from an illness, the quarantine period will necessarily lengthen until the tortoise has been treated successfully.

During the quarantine period, it is advisable to keep the habitat as sparsely decorated and simple as possible, while still providing for the animal's basic needs. Many reptile keepers prefer to keep

117

quarantined animals on a newspaper or paper towel substrate, which expedites the collection of stool samples. However, paper substrates are not appropriate for the long-term maintenance of Russian tortoises, so it is not applicable to this species. Feed, water and care for your tortoise as usual during the process, but keep everything simple to avoid compounding problems that may not yet be apparent.

During the quarantine period, your tortoise must have be inspected by a veterinarian. In all likelihood, the veterinarian will perform a physical examination, check a stool sample for parasite eggs and draw blood to assess any underlying infections or problems. In most cases, wild caught Russian tortoises will have more than one type of intestinal parasite, and they may have other problems as well.

Most parasite treatments require several treatments. Your veterinarian will likely administer a parasitic drug to your tortoise, and either show you how to administer a second dose or schedule another appointment to administer a follow-up dose. It is often advised to perform another fecal examination after two or three treatments and then proceed as necessary.

It is important to collect stool samples while they are fresh, and transport them to your veterinarian as soon as possible. If your tortoise reliably defecates in response to a given stimulus (such as being misted or lifted off the ground) you can collect the sample at the veterinarian's office. Always collect and store stool samples in a sealed plastic bag or container to keep them from dehydrating.

4. Legal Considerations

Russian tortoises are classified under Appendix II of the Convention on International Trade in Endangered Species (CITES). This means that in order to ship them across international boundaries, Russian tortoises must have an export permit from their country of origin.

Animals are assigned to a Cites appendix based on their status in the wild, and their potential for extinction. The IUCN Red List of Threatened Species lists Russian tortoises as "Vulnerable." Were they to be in greater peril, they would be listed on Appendix I. Appendix I animals require both export and import permits; such animals are not sold commercially. Appendix I animals include imperiled tortoises such as Madagascan and radiated tortoises. However, most common pet tortoises are listed as part of Appendix II.

For the average hobbyist, these regulations mean relatively little. Always purchase tortoises from reputable, licensed breeders or retailers to ensure the animals you purchase were legally obtained. However, if you plan to breed and sell your tortoises, you will need to investigate the laws, regulations and ordinances of your area. If you plan to ship internationally, you will need to acquire even more permits and licenses.

Chapter 11: Resources, Support and Further Reading

Learning about Russian tortoises is a life-long process. Even the best-educated experts are always seeking to understand these wonderful creatures more completely. To that end, you should always seek to learn as much as you can about Russian tortoises, as well as general turtle biology and reptile husbandry.

While books, websites and reptile-oriented associations are the primary ways to learn more about tortoises, they are not the only ways. On slow weekday mornings, zookeepers are often easy to spot working with their captives. Usually, such keepers are happy to share their incredibly vast knowledge with respectful visitors. Many zoos, nature centers and environmental education organizations maintain or otherwise work with tortoises – you may consider volunteering with such organizations to learn more about tortoises. If you think that you may want to make a career of working with tortoises, consider going to college and majoring in herpetology.

1. Books

Bookstores and online book retailers often offer a treasure trove of information that will help your quest for knowledge. While books represent an additional cost involved in turtle care, you can consider it an investment in your pet's wellbeing. Your local library may also carry some books about tortoises, which you can borrow for no charge. University libraries are a great place for finding old, obscure or academically oriented books about tortoises. You may not be allowed to borrow these books if you are not a student, but you can view and read them at the library.

It is important to check the date of the information provided in books. Russian tortoise husbandry is a relatively new phenomenon, and every bit of knowledge gained by scientists and keepers has the potential to revolutionize the current husbandry paradigm.

a) General Reptile Books

Herpetology: An Introductory Biology of Amphibians and Reptiles

By Laurie J. Vitt, Janalee P. Caldwell

Academic Press, 2013

This book will help beginners and advanced keepers alike to develop a better understanding of basic reptile biology.

Understanding Reptile Parasites: A Basic Manual for Herpetoculturists & Veterinarians

By Roger Klingenberg D.V.M.

Advanced Vivarium Systems, 1997

This book provides herpetoculturists with a basic understanding of the different types of parasites that are common in captive reptiles and the treatments that veterinarians commonly prescribe.

b) Turtle and Tortoise Books

Turtles of the World

By Franck Bonin, Bernard DeVaux, Alain Dupree and Peter C.H. Pritchard

Johns Hopkins University Press, 2006

This book is essential reading for anyone who wants to understand turtle diversity and natural history.

Turtles & Tortoises For Dummies

By Liz Palika

John Wiley & Sons, 2011

Covering most of the species commonly kept in captivity; this book provides basic information about turtles and tortoises in a simple, straightforward way.

Care for Your Pet Tortoise

V.T. 2014

Turtles, Tortoises and Terrapins: A Natural History

Ronald Orenstein

Firefly Books, 2012

Tortoise (Expert Series)

Lance Jepson

Magnet & Steel, 2012

The Conservation Biology of Tortoises

Edited by Ian Richard Swingland, Michael W. Klemens

IUCN--the World Conservation Union, 1989

c) Russian Tortoise Books

Russian Tortoises in Captivity

Jerry D. Fife

ECO Publishing, 2013

Russian Tortoises (Complete Herp Care)

E.J. Pirog

TFH Publications, Inc., 2012

Russian Tortoises: A Complete Guide to Testudo

E. J. Pirog 2009

2. Informative Websites, Message Boards and Forums

With the explosion of the Internet, tortoise information is more available than it ever has been. However, this growth has cause an increase in the proliferation of both good information and bad information. While knowledgeable breeders, keepers and academics, operate some websites, others lack the same dedication and scientific rigor. Anyone can launch a website and say virtually anything they want about Russian tortoises. Accordingly, as with all other research, consider the source of the information before making any husbandry decisions.

a) General Turtle and Tortoise Sites

Testudines – Tree of Life Web Project

http://tolweb.org

The Tree of Life Project is a collection of information that includes hundreds of species, written by experts in their respective fields. This particular page covers the group Testudines, which includes all living turtles, tortoises and sea turtles.

The Phylogeny of Turtles

http://research.amnh.org

This web page is part of the American Museum of Natural History, and it explains the current research and basics of the turtle family tree.

Kingsnake.com's Tortoise Forum

http://forums.kingsnake.com

Kingsnake.com is one of the largest message boards for reptiles, and the site's tortoise forum is a great place for tortoise enthusiasts to learn and exchange ideas. Although the site features discussion on all species of tortoises, many of the ideas that are shared are applicable to Russian tortoises.

b) Russian Tortoise Sites

Tortoise Forum Facebook Page

https://www.facebook.com

This page allows keepers to discuss all aspects of life with Russian tortoises. While it is open for discussion to all species, the page is specifically dedicated to Russian tortoises.

The Russian Tortoise Forum

http://www.tortoiseforum.org

This fun, light-hearted message board provides quality information and connects to forums about other tortoise species.

The Russian Tortoise

http://russiantortoise.net

This website contains information on the husbandry, natural history, diet and reproductive habits of Russian tortoises.

Austin's Turtle Page: Russian Tortoise Care Sheet

http://www.austinsturtlepage.com

Austin's Turtle Page is a repository for care sheet, natural history information and a discussion board for all turtle-related things.

Arkive: The Afghan Tortoise

http://www.arkive.org

This page presents information on the biology, natural history and reproductive habits of the Afghan tortoise (aka the Russian tortoise), as well as several photographs of the species.

Sexing Russian Tortoises

http://www.chelonia.org

This page was authored by the World Chelonia Group, and includes excellent, side-by-side photographs of male and female Russian tortoises.

About.com: Russian Tortoise

http://animals.about.com

This page provides information regarding natural history, biology and captive care for Russian tortoises.

iNaturalist: Afghan Tortoise

http://www.inaturalist.org

This page contains user-submitted information on Afghan (Russian) Tortoises.

IUCN Red List of Threatened Species: Testudo horsfieldii

http://www.iucnredlist.org

The IUCN Red List of Threatened Species serves as an index of the status of the world's various species.

The Reptile Database: Testudo horsfieldii

http://reptile-database.reptarium.cz

This page contains information on the wild status, subspecies, common names, synonyms and range of Russian tortoises. This page also includes a robust list of references that are relevant to the species.

Practical Care and Breeding of the Russian Tortoise in Captivity

http://www.tortoisetrust.org

This page is part of the Tortoise Trust web site, and it provides information for maintaining and breeding Russian tortoises.

Practical Care and Breeding of the Horsfield's (Russian) Tortoise in Captivity

http://www.anapsid.org

This page is part of Melissa Kaplan's "Herp Care Collection".

c) Central Asia Geographic and Climate Information

National Snow and Ice Data Center: Central Asia

http://nsidc.org

This website includes a large database containing climate information about Central Asia.

USA Today, Central Asia Weather

http://traveltips.usatoday.com

Though oriented for travelers, this site contains good information for Russian tortoise keepers.

3. Clubs and Organizations

One of the most fun ways to learn more about keeping Russian tortoises is by speaking with others that do just that! While tortoises are not as popular as dogs and cats, you may be surprised just how many people living in your area are also fond of tortoises.

While there are a few clubs dedicated specifically for turtle and tortoise keepers, general reptile clubs are more common. Many who keep snakes, lizards and other unusual pets have a soft spot for turtles as well. While it would be nice to meet a club composed exclusively of tortoise keepers, there is considerable value in speaking with keepers of other reptiles too. Many of the techniques, strategies and methods used for taking care of one type of reptile are applicable to other types of reptiles.

For example, keepers of diurnal, vegetarian lizards, such as green iguanas (*Iguana iguana*), use lights to provide their animals with vitamin D3 just as tortoise keepers do. Additionally, they often feed somewhat similar diets to their lizards as you do to your Russian tortoise.

Even if you cannot find other Russian tortoise aficionados, such as yourself, there is much to be learned from keepers of other tortoise species. In particular, keepers of pancake tortoises (*Malacochersus tornieri*), Mediterranean tortoises (*Testudo* sp.) and African spurred tortoises (*Geochelone sulcata*) may have a lot to offer.

While pancake tortoises are quite different from Russian tortoises, they are both relatively small species, so other keepers may have discovered products and techniques that are applicable to your tortoises. Alternatively, if you want to learn about burrowing behavior and how to provide your Russian tortoises with a good substrate, talk to a keeper who works with African spurred tortoises. Spurred tortoises are the third largest tortoises in the world, and they dig tunnels up to 30 feet long (9 meters)! After figuring out how to deal with the tunnels they create, the relatively tiny burrows of Russian tortoises should be no problem!

International Turtles Association

http://www.isv.cc

The International Turtles Association is an international club for turtle breeders, keepers and enthusiasts.

British Chelonia Group

http://www.britishcheloniagroup.org.uk

The British Chelonia Group seeks to aid keepers in providing quality care for their captives, help support turtle research and conservation and encourage the acquisition of captive bred – rather than wild caught – turtles.

Dutch Turtle and Tortoise Society

http://www.trionyx.nl

The Dutch Turtle and Tortoise Society maintains a website with a great deal of information, including a studbook of registered turtles and legal information.

4. Conservation Groups, Academic Institutions and Information

The Asian Turtle Program

http://www.asianturtleprogram.org

The Asian Turtle Program is a program designed to protect the native turtles of Southeast Asia, with an emphasis on the species native to Vietnam.

Chelonian Research Foundation

http://www.chelonian.org

Is a non-profit organization, founded in 1992 that seeks to support turtle-oriented scientific research, especially as it relates to their diversity and conservation biology.

Journal of the Chelonian Research Foundation

http://www.chelonianjournals.org

The Chelonian Research Foundation publishes scientific information in journal form.

Society for the Study of Reptiles and Amphibians

http://www.ssarherps.org

The SSAR is a non-profit group committed to advancing the study of reptiles and amphibians. This group publishes the "Journal of Herpetology," and well as several other reptile-related publications.

5. Veterinarians, Health Resources and Husbandry Supplies

Association of Reptile and Amphibian Veterinarians

http://www.arav.org

This page includes a searchable database of veterinarians who are qualified to treat reptiles and amphibians.

AfricanTortoise.com: Toxic Plants and Flowers

http://africantortoise.com

An overview of plants and flowers that are thought to be toxic to turtles.

Avian and Exotic Animal Care: Houseplants That Are Safe for Herbivorous Reptiles

http://avianandexotic.com

Tired of looking at lists containing hundreds of plants that are probably poisonous? Check out this list of plants that are known to be safe for most herbivorous reptiles.

Melissa Kaplan's Herp Care Collection: Edible Plants

http://www.anapsid.org

Another resource that lists plants that are known to be safe for reptiles to consume.

California Turtle and Tortoise Club: Poisonous Plant List

http://www.tortoise.org

Very helpful site for learning about the plants widely thought to be poisonous for turtles.

ASPCA's List of Toxic and Non-Toxic Plants

http://www.aspca.org

Although this page is geared towards dogs, cats and horses, it is a helpful resource to consult.

The Humane Society of the United States: Plants Potentially Poisonous to Pets

http://www.humanesociety.org

Another page primarily directed at dog and cat owners, but a valuable resource, nonetheless.

Big Apple Pet Supply

http://www.bigappleherp.com

Big Apple Pet Supply carries most common husbandry equipment, including heating devices, food dishes and supplements.

LLLReptile

http://www.lllreptile.com

LLL Reptile carries a wide variety of husbandry tools, heating devices, lighting products and more.

Doctors Foster and Smith

http://www.drsfostersmith.com

Foster and Smith is a veterinarian-owned retailer that supplies husbandry-related items to pet keepers. Additionally, their website features a wealth of information about reptile keeping and Russian tortoises.

References

Ellen Hitschfeld, E. H. (2008). Phalangeal formulae and ontogenetic variation of carpal morphology. *Amphibia-Reptilia*.

Fre´de´ric Lagarde, X. B. (2003). Foraging behaviour and diet of an ectothermic herbivore: Testudo. *ECOGRAPHY*.

Frédéric Lagarde, X. B. (2002). A short spring before a long jump: the ecological challenge to the steppe tortoise (Testudo horsfieldi) . *Canadian Journal of Zoology*.

http://russiantortoise.net/hibernation_journey.htm. (1997). *THE HIBERNATION JOURNEY*. Retrieved from The Russian Tortoise: http://russiantortoise.net/hibernation_journey.htm

IUCN Red List of Threatened Species. (2014). *Testudo horsfieldii*. Retrieved from IUCN Red List of Threatened Species: http://www.iucnredlist.org/details/21651/0

Marcela Buchtová, L. P. (2009). Complex Sensory Corpuscles in the Upper Jaw of Horsfield's Tortoise . *Acta Veterinaria Scandinavica*.

Uwe Fritz, M. A. (2009). Mitochondrial diversity of the widespread Central Asian steppe tortoise (Testudo horsfieldii Gray, 1844): implications for taxonomy and relocation of confiscated tortoises. *Amphibia-Reptilia*.

X. Bonnet, F. L. (2008). Sexual dimorphism in steppe tortoises (Testudo horsfieldii): influence of the environment and sexual selection on body shape and mobility. *Biological Journal of the Linnean Society*.

Index

Afghan tortoises, 13
Anorexia, 106, 107
bacteria, 29, 92, 105, 106
bleach, 60, 61, 83
Breeders, 114
Breeding, 127
brumate, 41
bulbs, 39, 50, 51, 52, 53, 57, 61, 110
burrow, 44, 54, 57, 98
captive bred, 113
Captive bred, 113, 114
climate, 22
collapses, 59
Conservation, 123, 129
CRI, 50, 52, 53
density, 26
Depression, 106
dishes, 39, 60, 61, 83, 102
diurnal, 26
enclosures, 44, 52
Flowers, 71, 130
habitats, 26, 44, 51, 52, 58, 82
Health, 105
heating, 30, 31, 34, 40, 41, 46, 51, 53, 55, 56, 57, 60, 102, 110
husbandry, 10, 11, 33, 39, 86, 93, 104, 105, 106, 110, 121, 122, 124, 125, 131
Hygiene, 91

hyperparathyroidism, 109, 110
incubator, 99
Indoor, 45, 54
infections, 105, 106
Legal, 119
length, 18
Lethargy, 106
lighting, 30, 31, 34, 40, 49, 51, 60, 102, 109, 110
markings, 14
Mediterranean tortoises, 13, 128
metabolic, 109, 110
nails, 15
Non-Toxic, 131
online, 104, 114, 117, 121
Outdoor, 40, 42
pancake tortoises, 128
Parasite, 107
Pets, 29, 87, 131
Poisonous, 130, 131
predators, 42, 43, 111
price, 113, 114, 115, 117
Rocks, 59
Russian box turtles, 13
salmonella, 29
scales, 15
scutes, 60, 94
Sexing, 126
shell, 13, 18, 59, 94, 95, 99, 102, 109
shipping, 102, 117

sick, 35, 91, 104, 106, 111,
113, 117
spot cleaning, 30
subspecies, 21, 126
substrate, 39, 44, 45, 46, 53,
55, 57, 58, 59, 60, 61, 98,
102, 106, 112, 128
Substrate, 32, 57
TDSD, 100
temperature, 36, 52, 53, 54,
55, 56, 57, 64, 65, 83, 96,
99, 100, 106
Testudo, 13, 20, 21, 124,
126, 128

thermometer, 39, 54
Toxic, 74, 75, 130, 131
trough, 46, 49
tubs, 46
ultraviolet radiation, 52
UV, 50, 51, 52
Veterinarians, 130
Vomiting, 107
Vulnerable, 22, 120
water, 30, 46, 56, 60, 61, 81,
82, 83, 91, 98, 99, 102
wild caught, 95, 113, 115,
116, 129

Published by IMB Publishing 2014

CPSIA information can be obtained at www.ICGtesting.com
Printed in the USA
BVOW06s2142240716

456590BV00006B/54/P